D1590106

SHAKESPEARIAN COSTUME
FOR STAGE AND SCREEN

PLATE I

Doublet with large buttons, trunk sleeves, flat wings, small skirt; falling band and cuffs; decorated girdle and sidepiece of hangers; French cloak; ear-ring. *c.* 1580-85.

Sir Walter Raleigh; unknown artist. *National Portrait Gallery, London.*

F. M. KELLY

Shakespearian Costume for Stage and Screen

COMPLETELY REVISED BY
ALAN MANSFIELD

ADAM & CHARLES BLACK
LONDON

FIRST PUBLISHED 1938
SECOND EDITION, REVISED AND RESET 1970
REPRINTED WITH CORRECTIONS 1973

A. & C. BLACK LIMITED
4, 5 AND 6 SOHO SQUARE LONDON W1V 6AD

ISBN 0 7136 10468

PRINTED IN GREAT BRITAIN
BY T. & A. CONSTABLE LTD., EDINBURGH

Contents

		PAGE
	PREFACE	9
CHAPTER		
I	GENERAL INTRODUCTION	11
II	MEN'S CLOTHES, 1570–1620	21
III	WOMEN'S CLOTHES, 1570–1620	47
IV	I FOREIGN CHARACTERISTICS	61
	II ARMOUR	64
V	ON THE "NICE CONDUCT" OF PERIOD COSTUME	77
VI	THE PLAYS	89
	I The Histories	89
	II The Tragedies	93
	III The Comedies	98
VII	ON AVAILABLE SOURCES AND THEIR SELECTION	106
VIII	ODDS AND ENDS	110
	GENERAL BIBLIOGRAPHY	114
	INDEX	119

Plates

PLATE		FACING PAGE
1	Sir Walter Raleigh	*frontispiece*
2	Sir Philip Sidney	16
3	Philip II of Spain in armour	33
4	Nobleman of the 1560's	48
5	Sir Phineas Pett	65
6	Queen Elizabeth I	80
7	Woman's jacket and skirt c. 1610	97
8	Mary, Queen of Scots	112

Preface to the Revised Edition

At first sight the revision of such a classic as this book may seem an impertinence. I hope, however, that I am not so guilty.

In the thirty-odd years since this work first appeared we have experienced among other things a second world war, the rise of television, and a revolution in modes and manners, which have affected the Theatre and Screen no less than they have most other aspects of society.

One of the developments in the field of history and the arts is the study of historic costume in greater detail than ever before, and the post-war years have seen the fruition of the works of Drs C. Willett and Phillis Cunnington, Mr James Laver, and a host of other specialists too numerous to name in this preface.

In addition, the costume collections of our national and local museums and galleries have been receiving greater attention and study, and the Gallery of English Costume in Manchester and the Gallery of Costume now housed in Bath have added immeasurably to our sources of practical knowledge. An immensely greater selection of authoritative works on costume is now available than was to Mr Kelly, including excellent books on the construction, and no less important, the wearing of period clothes. These additions to the literature of the subject are reflected in the extended bibliography.

Contemporary written and pictorial sources are also now easier to come by, and a new selection of illustrations has been made for this edition, based on English originals, backed where necessary with examples from the Continent.

The sections of the original edition analysing male and female dress have been expanded into two chapters, and features of foreign clothes collected in Chapter IV together with the notes on armour.

The section on costuming the plays has been slightly added to, and some illustrations included.

Mr Kelly's knowledge of both armour and the Theatre was such that little revision has been attempted ; in the latter case, such additions and excisions only as are necessary to suit the text to a new generation of readers have been made.

I have not included any quotations or references in the text as this book is intended for the busy producer, director and designer rather than the historian; ample contemporary evidence can be found quoted in the works of Linthicum, Laver and the Cunningtons.

My gratitude for help, advice and encouragement is due to my wife, who is also responsible for the new illustrations, to Dr Phillis Cunnington, and to the staffs of those libraries and museums and theatres I have consulted, especially the Colchester Borough Library, the London Museum, the National Portrait Gallery, The Royal Shakespeare Theatre, The National Theatre, and the Colchester Mercury Theatre; also to Mr A. Rubens, who first published the illustrations shown at figs. 47, 48 and 49 in his "History of Jewish Costume". Mrs Ralph Luckham and the printers earn well-deserved praise for coping with my handwriting. Lastly, I must thank Mr A. Black for entrusting this revision to me.

The responsibility for the revised portions of this work is, however, mine alone, and all shortcomings are to be laid at my door.

WEST MERSEA,
1968-69, and 1973 A. D. M.

CHAPTER I

GENERAL INTRODUCTION

How should Shakespeare's plays be costumed and mounted? For my own part, I propose to limit myself to costume alone, a department of stage (and film) production which might well give scope to a far more ambitious effort than the present work. Even in this single particular *quot homines, tot sententiae*, and for most views a more or less plausible case can be made out. It is no use appealing in the last resort to Shakespeare himself. Of Montaigne an excellent French antiquary has said with some truth, "*il a touché à tout*", and our national vanity might prompt us to retort, "What price Shakespeare then?" None of his gifts is taken more for granted than his astounding universality. Yet when we fall back upon his writings for evidence of the *appearance* of his characters in their habits as they live, we have to confess that he is less circumstantial than almost any of his fellow-dramatists. Had he shown more interest in details of the outer man, were he richer in such touches as enliven, say, Jonson, this question of a fitting wardrobe would hardly be the moot point it has become.

On the other hand even in this respect he has a good deal more to tell us than most critics seem to have troubled to find out. Which is all the more surprising in view of the colossal bibliography that has grown up round him, his works and every conceivable topic directly or indirectly bearing on them. Even the Furnival *Variorum* edition is strangely disappointing in this respect. The subject of arms and armour by the way receives in the plays even less attention than costume, which is odd when we consider how prominent a part is played in them by warfare and armed violence. But in this respect he is by no means singular, and one is tempted to conjecture that the paucity of his armour-vocabulary merely reflects a fast-growing unfamiliarity with such matters on the part of the average stay-at-home Englishman. Be that as it may, in war or peace Shakespeare has done little enough to familiarize us with the appearance of the men he moved among, and if it is these we aim at reviving on stage or screen, we must draw our own information from a different source. The requisite knowledge must come from extensive and intensive study of independent first-hand documents both literary and pictorial, which must be very carefully compared. Above all, we must never neglect to verify our references at the source wherever possible.

But the methods adopted nowadays vary greatly and each has its champions. It is probably fair to say that two-thirds of any average audience—and it is these after all that constitute our final court of appeal—have no very rooted prejudice one way or the other.

Let us consider the various methods in vogue in our day for costuming Shakespeare. These are to employ :

1. A vaguely mediaeval convention conceived in the spirit of a provincial carnival.

2. Appropriate period-costume.

3. A setting in what one assumes to be the spirit of the original performances.

4. The style of the author's own day.

5. The fashions of the present day.

Of these I think best to deal with the last first, for the sake of getting it out of the way. In 1973 a Stratford production of *As You Like It* could exploit the contemporary dress of shirt and slacks, common to both sexes, in Rosalind's masquerade, but at least one critic doubted its efficacy. Can such productions fit the circumstances—can " doublet and hose " be " courageous to petticoat " in these conditions ? I scarcely think my pleasure would have been enhanced by the up-to-date setting. I am familiar with all the stock arguments : Shakespeare knew nothing and cared less—how do we know whether he cared ?—about " period " ; Betterton, Garrick, Mrs Siddons were supreme exponents of the leading rôles and they were content with the dress of their own day. The practice of Shakespeare's own day we will return to presently. Let us for the moment deal with the second argument. Now in the first place this requires to be strongly qualified. As far as Garrick is concerned he certainly played Hamlet in a black velvet court-suit and powdered wig, Macbeth in the uniform of the footguards, etc. (Fig. 1), and this was the general rule before and after his time. On the other hand even he made notable exceptions : his Richard III was attired in what then was assumed to be " mediaeval " costume. So was his Don John in *The Changeling*. Mrs Siddons introduced a number of fanciful modifications of current modes into many of her parts. Moreover there were a number of Shakespearian rôles

—Viola, Sir Andrew, Falstaff—whom it seems to have been agreed to costume in the "Gothick" spirit (Fig. 2). I have not room here to labour the point. But even if every actor from Burbage to Garrick had dressed Shakespeare from the resources of his personal wardrobe, that would not justify the present generation in seeking to follow their example;

1. Garrick as Macbeth, 1775.
Contemporary print.

2. Phelps as Falstaff, 1846.
He is dressed in the "Gothick" or Holbein style said to have been introduced by Garrick.
Contemporary print.

since in the mere externals of life there is far more in common between Burbage and Garrick than between either of them and the present day. In the 18th century, for instance, the sword had not yet become an abnormal or alien element in ordinary life: it is as remote from our industrial culture as motors from the Middle Ages. But in play after play of Shakespeare the vital essence of the plot requires a sword to be worn as a matter of course. Take for instance all that business of the Capulet-Montague vendetta in *Romeo and Juliet,* culminating in the deaths of Mercutio and Tybalt: how does that accord with a 20th-century *milieu*? No doubt the incongruity could be circumvented ; but is it worth while to expend so much ingenuity for the sake of wearing our very unpicturesque modern attire ? And if so, where do you propose to draw the line ? Will you, for the sake of being " modern ", turn Samson, Gregory, Abraham and Balthasar into rival gunmen ?

Next we come to the proposal to treat *all* the plays indiscriminately in the costume of the latter half of the 16th century or the opening years of the 17th. This, I believe, was the late William Poel's ideal. I believe that at Stratford *Troilus and Cressida* was produced on these lines before the Second World War : the result would seem to have been highly picturesque. But it will only be justified if you are consistent throughout. Your costumes and properties in each play must conform to their Elizabethan prototypes down to the smallest detail—or rather there must be no *perceptible* discrepancy. This means that you must saturate yourself in the taste of the period. The present volume having no pretence to be a comprehensive history of costume from Timon of Athens to Henry VIII, or later, has attempted at least to detail at some length the principal modes familiar to Shakespeare and his contemporaries. There can be no doubt that at any rate a considerable proportion of the plays lend themselves perfectly to an Elizabethan treatment, and the descriptions in Chapters II, III and IV together with the illustrations should assist the producer to realize this object. It would be mere conceit to pretend it exhausts the subject, or does more than guide the student's feet in the direction sought, pointing out the essential landmarks. You have the further practical advantage, if you adopt 16th century throughout, of being able to use a great part of your wardrobe for any play—especially for minor rôles.

Follows the proposal to put on your plays in accordance with the (presumed) methods of Shakespeare's time.

I shall doubtless be told that this is essentially the course described in the foregoing paragraph. Doubtless that is true *up to a point.* It is, however, probably by no means so true as it would have been of the mediaeval mystery-plays. The art of the Middle Ages presented the events of the Old Testament, of classical antiquity and the past generally, in the guise familiar to the artist and his contemporaries. God and His angels, the Saviour, His Mother and Apostles have from a remote date been depicted in a stereotyped fashion that stamp them apart. Evil spirits too are unmistakable. Otherwise there was little or nothing in the characters portrayed to mark period or nation. With the Renaissance, however, there was a growing tendency in masques and pageants to distinguish allegorical persons, " Turks " and the like, and even to introduce an " antick " element into pagans generally. No longer were Alexander or Scipio pictured as feudal knights. The Shakespearian " clown ", as opposed to the professional " fool ", was probably something of a figure of fun, a caricature rather than a true copy of the yokel of the period : in fact " the comic countryman " of the Vincent Crummles tradition. I very much doubt whether we are yet sufficiently well informed about Shakespearian stage-conventions to hope to reproduce them faithfully. One can but recognize the fact that the

3. The earliest known Shakespeare illustration, *Titus Andronicus*, 1594.
Contemporary and " antick " clothes.
Drawing by Henry Peacham, 1594. (Marquis of Bath's collection.)

original costume of the plays was that of the author's day, more or less tempered by a conventional antique or satiric note : a mixture of actuality and mere fancy-dress (Fig. 3).

As for the type of costume which heads our list—the vaguely " mediaeval " or carnival type long dear to amateur dramatic societies and the old touring companies in " number two " towns, it is perhaps more convincing than the most " modern " productions applauded by our intelligentsia. There is in both cases a danger of their being conceived in the spirit of Mr Winkle's " regular, authentic, every-day costume of a Troubadour " vouched for by Solomon Lucas of Eatanswill (*Pickwick Papers*, chap. XV). Much as our futurist designer may chafe at the comparison, there is a good deal in common between him and the Solomon Lucases of our day, in that both are a law unto themselves and not to be judged by antecedent probability. As such one cannot demand of them to " abide our question ".

Remains the suggestion of adhering to appropriate period costumes and "props". The word to stress here is "appropriate": apart from the definitely historical plays, each of the pieces requires to be taken on its merits. Clearly here is a point which calls for much discretion as well as a sound knowledge of the trappings of past ages. There is always a tendency to dress one's shop-window over-lavishly. One is apt to seize the opportunity of parading one's erudition by giving undue prominence to the unfamiliar for its own sake. The great thing to remember if you decide to go in for period is that nothing must belie the spirit of the time and place[1] you decide on. So long as the prevalent *character* is never lost sight of, there is no call to insist on mere eccentricities, still less to cramp your actor's style by hampering his freedom of action. Remember that your costume can never at best be more than a convincing fake, heightening the illusion produced by fine acting: it must be a help, not a hindrance. Here the ingenuity of your costumier and the good will of your actor can be of priceless assistance. You cannot know too much about your period: the wider your knowledge the greater your field of selection. As long ago as 1860 Fairholt could say, "False costume is now an unnecessary obtrusion, and not worth an excuse". How much more true of the present day when the amount of material sifted and rendered available for general consumption has multiplied a hundred-fold! It is the more extraordinary that so few designers of historical subjects seem to take any pains to keep abreast of the ever-increasing flood of first-hand evidence incessantly placed at their disposal. The worst exaggerations of fashion are best reserved for comic fops or introduced as high lights amid a crowd of "courtiers" or the like. In many cases they must be toned down or even omitted altogether. The greater your practical experience in such matters the more rarely will you find real difficulty in coping with seemingly awkward details.

The difficulty with some costumiers is that they will insist on making the dress of past ages conform to the basic principles of modern tailoring, whereas it is of the first importance that they should learn to adapt their craft to the fashions of a given period. The result is seldom edifying. Where the tailor has on the other hand penetrated the secrets of old-time cut, the effect is not only convincing but often unexpectedly practical. It can hardly be too often repeated that the secret of effective costume is that of a perfectly fitting modern suit: a matter of correct cut.

[1] I mention "place" because the "Illyria", "Bohemia", "Athens", etc., of the plays is not always to be taken seriously.

PLATE 2

Peascod-bellied doublet, slashed and pinked, plain wings, very small skirt; gorget; ruff and ruffles set in figures-of-eight; bombasted and paned trunkhose with cod-piece: sidepiece of hangers passed through panes of trunkhose. *c.* 1577.

Sir Philip Sidney; unknown artist.
National Portrait Gallery, London.

In the 1960's many productions earnestly strive to " relate " Shakespeare to the political and social perplexities which are assumed to be peculiar to this age, and for this reason underline the timeless qualities of the plays by, among other means, a deliberately vague dressing of neither our nor Shakespeare's day, or by placing the action and costume in an alien era—the nearer past or the problematic future, or by freely interpreted 16th-century designs which do not attempt any accuracy of costuming.

It is perhaps fair to say that for every member of an audience who appreciates such interpretations another one would gain as much from a more traditional treatment, dressed in the costume of the playwright's day or in an honest attempt to bring to the stage the historic clothes of the age in which the play is set.

But whatever his outlook and however he attempts to achieve his aim, let the designer always remember the words of Voltaire :

All styles are good except the tiresome sort.

NOTES

COLOURS. The importance of black in the collective colour-scheme of Elizabethan costume is apt to be underestimated. Omitting on the one hand the clergy, scholars and professional men (who wore black almost as a prescriptive right) and on the other the working classes (whose apparel was largely " self-coloured " and variegated) it is probably safe to say that black would be the dominant note in any average Elizabethan crowd. As a pre-eminently " respectable " colour, all-black was unimpeachable wear, and as such equally suitable to all pretenders to gentility from the highest in the land to the shabby-genteel. Its widespread vogue was favoured alike by Puritan gravity and the austerity of Catholic Spain. Even without any relief of gold or silver a complete suit of black velvet was fit apparel for a king. Even where other colours were worn, comparatively few suits of apparel were wholly free from some admixture of black.

Brocades, cloth of gold and of silver were only worn by the greatest on occasions of state. No colour was in greater vogue at court than white, then follow red (scarlet, rose, crimson), yellow (primrose to deep saffron), purple (murrey, violet), green and grey. Throughout the reign of Elizabeth a certain uniformity prevailed in fashionable attire. The taste of the period prescribed a harmony of (usually) not more than two colours.

By the latter part of the reign white and silver was in great favour at court. A similar restraint is observable at the French court till 1575, after which the opposite extravagance was the rule, the utmost variety of colouring being aimed at in modish costume, each article of attire contrasting with its neighbour.

4. John Tradescant I. Jerkin worn open over doublet; Venetians; copotain hat. *c.* 1611.
Carving at Hatfield House.

A startling exception was the vogue for ordinary wear of all-green costumes set by the Duke of Alençon (afterwards of Anjou, the notorious suitor of our Queen Elizabeth): this had to be uniform from top to toe. It seems to have been practically confined to France.

Something of the same polychromatic taste, though rather less pronounced, reigned at the English court under James I.

Where—as in the majority of cases—a definite harmony was aimed at, the almost universal rule is for the upper garment to be of a darker tone than the under. Caps and (where of a textile material) hats are nearly always black, the cloak generally so, jerkins (unless of leather) likewise of a dark colour. By "*suit* of apparel" is meant an *ensemble* of like material, colour and decoration. The hose usually match the doublet; less commonly the jerkin, when the doublet is of a plain light colour mostly to match the stockings.

Blue—in England at least—was a distinctly unfashionable colour. It was the recognized colour of apprentices, of servants' livery and soldiers' regulation coats. People of quality therefore looked on it with no great favour.

> Where exceptions occur—as in Isaac Oliver's well-known miniatures of the Earl of Dorset and Lord Howard of Cherbury—the wearing of blue seems to have a definite military character. Note too that these examples belong to the 17th century when the Elizabethan conventions had been relaxed.

A remark seems justified here *à propos* of military privileges. Previous to our age of khaki, the uniforms of the army were the one bright spot in a drab industrial world. Note that at all times bright colours and showy trimmings have marked out the man of war.[1] In Shakespeare's time too the sumptuary laws were considerably relaxed in favour of military men, who were only too ready to interpret their privileges with extreme latitude, as were others whose military qualifications were of the slenderest. Moreover not all " gentlemen " in the army held commissions. Many contented themselves with trailing a pike or shouldering an arquebuse as " gentlemen of a company " fighting in the front ranks on double pay.

It is well to realize that the sumptuary edicts were—as in most ages—more numerous than effective.

FASTENINGS. It is worth while to remember how varied are the methods by which the clothes were adjusted to the person: points, buttons—either with buttonholes or loops—or hooks and eyes. The position of the necessary openings also differed: front, sides or back. Jerkins in particular were often made to pull over the head like a shirt, when they could be fastened at the breast, and up the sides. For their nicer fit they could be further provided with extra slits made to button up.

CUTS, SLASHES and PULLINGS OUT. The generic term for the ornamental perforations in clothes seems to have been *cuts*; *slashes* properly denoting the elongated slits so favoured in Germany. Except where German modes prevailed, this cutting and slashing was rarely on such a scale as materially to affect the general outline. Very long slashes are noticeable especially on jerkins and the body of women's gowns. By *pinking* is implied minute perforations such as might be made by an awl or stiletto. The *slashes* were often lined with thin silk, which could be " drawn forth " in puffs through the slits, and are referred to in contemporary writings as *pullings out.* In Germany these drawn-out puffs are emphasized to excess.

STRIPED EFFECTS. These are much used at this date to emphasize the lines of the figure. Striped fabrics, appliqués, even the pattern of the quilting and slashing were contrived to enhance this effect. Thus the lines of decoration on the trunk when disposed lengthwise generally radiated upward and downward from the girdlestead. When arranged obliquely they formed chevrons. But quite as often the striping ran

[1] " Bravery " then signified outward display as well as valour.

horizontally as on our footmen's waistcoats. Sleeves were very generally striped across.

GUARDS. Were broad bands of ribbon-like material used chiefly as trimming along the edges and seams of a garment and across the hanging sleeves ; especially in liveries and military and official dress.

POINTS. There is in principle no difference between *points* and our shoe-laces, except in length. The tags were called *aglets.* Originally points served a purely utilitarian end as mere fastenings. In the 16th century they were often highly decorative and were largely used as a mere ornamental garnish, the laces being of broad, coloured riband and the *aglets* large and beautifully wrought in goldsmith's work. In accordance with 16th-century practice, when not designed to be in evidence, they were perfectly plain but strong. This would be the case usually with the points used for bracing up the hose, or securing portions of the armour. The *vambraces,* for instance, when not united to the *pauldrons,* were attached to points at the shoulders of the *arming-doublet* (see page 65).

YOUNG MEN IN LOVE. "A sweet disorder in the dress" was symbolically indicative that a young man was in love. His points or buttons were left undone, his hat-band forgotten, or some other sartorial negligence was made self-evident. See *As You Like It,* Act 3, Sc 2.

CHAPTER II

MEN'S CLOTHES, 1570-1620

"You bid me make it orderly and well
According to the fashion of the time."
Taming of the Shrew, IV, iii

The burly aggressive characteristics of Tudor male modes began to soften about the middle of the 16th century and as the reign of Elizabeth I developed so did fashions unconsciously become influenced by the femininity of the Queen and her court, where the farthingale seemed to take pride of place and the male silhouette declined from the squarely stout to the taperingly slender—even to the extent of exhibiting an hour-glass figure of quite womanly proportions. Under James I this silhouette gradually altered again, until about 1630, the tight-laced corset shape of the doublet was replaced by easy fitting, higher waisted versions.

The principal male garments of the period were doublet, hose, gown and cloak. Other garments were also in evidence, notably the jerkin. During the period we are considering the cloak was gaining in popularity, replacing the earlier gown, which latter by 1600 had become, generally speaking, a mark of the professional man.

It was considered unbecoming for a gentleman to appear in public in doublet and hose alone, or even in doublet, hose and jerkin—that is, in the phrase of the day, "*in querpo*". A gown or cloak was essential out of doors, and frequently worn indoors as well, especially on formal occasions, when the hat also was retained. When dancing, the cloak was discarded but the hat was usually kept on.

To satisfy good manners the cloak could be carried over the arm instead of being worn.

At Court, all but liveried servants, guards, etc., were expected to wear gown or cloak, though, of course, heads were bared in the Royal Presence.

A further mark of gentility was the wearing of a sword out of doors; or having it carried behind one by a servant.

THE DOUBLET. This was to its day what the jacket is to modern man, making, with hose, and perhaps a waistcoat under, or jerkin over, the equivalent of the suit of today. During most of our period the doublet was close-fitting with a tight waist coming to a point in front (Pl. 1), which was most common up to 1590, or, from that date, tending to be displaced by a round waist (Pl. 5). The body of the doublet was padded, and stiffened with canvas or buckram in most cases, with pasteboard or busks as an added reinforcement in front. Extra padding in front was fashionable from 1575 to 1590, subsequently becoming less so. The " peascod belly ", a Dutch fashion, where excessive padding at the point of the waist caused an overhanging bulge, in extreme cases reaching down to the fork, was popular in this country from 1575 to 1600 (Pl. 2). The padding used to bear out the doublet was known as bombast (a word today defined as " inflated talk "), and was made of horsehair, flock, wool, rags, bran or cotton.

The effect aimed at was a small waist; the cut of the doublet, a tight fit, and the concentration of padding above and below the waistline all contributed to this effect.

The Collar. Throughout the period a standing collar was the usual mode. The years 1560–70 saw the maximum height, when it rose as high as the ears in some cases ; after 1570 the height lessened, or the collar was cut away in a slope to the front, to allow room for the large ruffs of the following decade, which were worn tilted up at the back (Fig. 5). Such standing collars could be plain, or topped with stiffened tabs, known as " pickadils ", turned out at right angles. Pickadils were partly ornament and partly supports for the ruff. Later, separate pickadils were worn. Occasionally between about 1590 and 1600, a narrow band, or plain round neck, with a small V in front, is seen.

The Skirt. The doublet skirt at this time was very short (Pl. 1.) : during the decade 1575-85 it became a mere border almost concealed by the girdle. It was flared, and stood out over the bombasted trunk hose, hiding the " points ", attaching the hose to the doublet. Skirts could be plain, or " wrought in pickadil ", that is slit into tabs, sometimes looped. From about 1590 the skirt might be made of separate rhomboidal flaps or tabs overlapping backwards (Fig. 7). From about 1610 the tabs were deeper and came down to a sharp point at the front.

The front edge, when plain or pickadiled, might meet flush or have a Λ gap or, up to 1580, overlap. The skirt of separate tabs met edge to edge, or perhaps overlapped in the case of a diagonal cut.

Fastenings. The doublet was fastened from the neck to the waist by one of the following methods : a close row of buttons with button holes or loops ; hooks and eyes ; lacing ; or by points or ties. Buttons were the most usual fastenings. By the end of the 16th century ordinary hooks and eyes had become cheaper and more popular : by the rich and noble silver

5. Two courtiers ; jerkins ; compound ruffs ; trunk-hose with canions; stockings with garters tied above knee ; short full, very decorated cloak. The left-hand figure has the insignia of the Order of the Garter. *c.* 1590.
Detail from a painting by Marcus Gheeraerts.
Wingfield Digby Collection.

ones were used (the Queen herself used vast quantities of these useful gadgets for her dresses).

Sleeves. Throughout the period close-fitting sleeves with eight or a dozen buttons at the wrist, closing a short vertical opening, were popular, as were, from 1575, " cannon " or " trunk " sleeves, which were wide from the shoulders, narrowing down to the wrist, and full " bishop " sleeves with a closed wrist-band. These last two types were distended by bombast, or by an undersleeve, or by wire, reed or whalebone stiffening. They were generally known as "farthingale sleeves" (Fig. 6). A variation, from about 1580, was the moderate full sleeve, narrowing to the wrist and with the front seam left open and secured by buttons or ties to expose in the gaps the white shirt sleeve, or doublet lining.

With all these types of sleeve, wings were almost always worn. One of the functions of the wing was to conceal the fastening at the armhole of detachable sleeves. Any type of sleeve might be detachable, secured to

6. Sleeveless jerkin with points as fastenings, closed at neck only, wings in pickadil; doublet with a modified trunk sleeve; Venetians fastened to doublet by concealed points, two of which, however, are visible, pickadils at knees. 1577.
Sir Martin Frobisher, Cornelis Ketel. Bodleian Library, Oxford.

the doublet body by points or buttons, but the doublet was never worn without sleeves in polite society. The wings were stiffened welts, and during the period under review were mostly a plain flat welt, a double row of flat looped tabs, or a plain undivided broad projection (Fig. 7; Pl. 2), and were made of the doublet material, stiffened with buckram, etc. A variation was the "roll", again of stiff buckram covered with doublet material and slashed into sections.

The material of the doublet ranged from velvet and satin to canvas and leather: the sleeves, if detachable, might be of different material and colour from the body, which itself often differed from the rest of the costume. Decoration might take the form of slashing, pinking or embroidery, including embroidery with pearls and jewels. Slashing was the cutting of slits in a garment, revealing the underclothes or a contrasting lining. In the 16th and most of the 17th centuries " pinking " denoted small slits or holes cut in symmetric designs in a garment. Two and a half or three yards of material was required, plus lining, lace, etc.

A girdle or waistband, narrow, and following the curve of the waistline (known as the " girdlestead "), could be worn with doublet or jerkin (Pls. 1 and 2). Often of leather, it could be silk, gold or silver, embroidered and jewelled for dress wear, or of a woven tape like material, caddis, for poorer people. Leather girdles were often fitted with a pair of hangers, to support sword or dagger. A purse, or in the case of clerkly persons, a pen-case and inkhorn, might be suspended from the girdle.

The lower garments—hose or breeches—were held up by ties or points threaded through eyelet holes in the lining of the doublet at the waistline, where the lining was generally strengthened by canvas. These eyelet holes and the points were, up to 1595, concealed by the doublet skirt, but after that date the holes sometimes pierced the doublet body itself, just above the skirt at the waist, and the points were tied on the outside (Figs. 6 and 7).

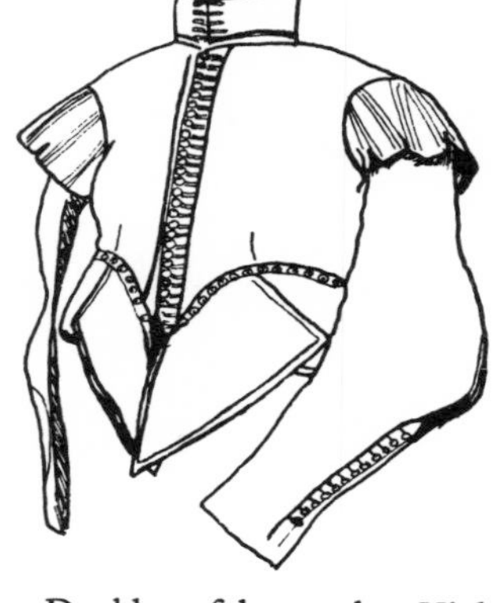

7. Doublet of late style. High-standing collar, wide, flat, tabbed wings, deep skirt in rhomboidal tabs, overlapping in front, buttoned sleeves, eyelet holes for trussing points at waist. *c.* 1620's.
Victoria & Albert Museum, London.

HOSE and BREECHES. Trunkhose, of two main types, either round, onion-shaped (1555–1570's), or in the shape of a truncated cone from waist to mid-thigh (1570–1610 approximately), were being replaced by various styles of breeches worn with separate stockings, during our period.

Trunkhose (trunk-slops, trunk breeches, trunks, round hose, or French hose) were a variety of whole-hose, or long-stocked hose, combining breeches and stockings in one garment (Pl. 3). The stockings were tailored, cut on the cross to fit smoothly, not knitted : they could be of a different colour and material from the breeches part. Until the mid 16th century the upper part, or breech, was known as the " upper stocks ", a name which died out to be replaced by the restriction of the word " hose " to this portion. The lower leg portion was known as the " nether stocks ", a name continuing until the end of the century. Between the two main types of trunkhose mentioned above many variations of cut existed.

An intermediate style of lower garment was that of trunkhose with " canions ". These were worn, like breeches proper, with separate stockings, but were cut on the lines of the truncated-cone type of trunkhose. Instead of full-length nether stocks, the leg portion terminated about knee level; these thigh-fitting portions, extensions only, as it were, of the breech, were known as " canions ", and separate stockings (tailored, or later, knitted) were either pulled up over them, above the knees, or the canions, if wide enough, could be fastened over the stockings, below the knee (Figs. 5 and 11). Canions were more often than not of a different material and colour from the trunkhose to which they were attached, and they were always lined.

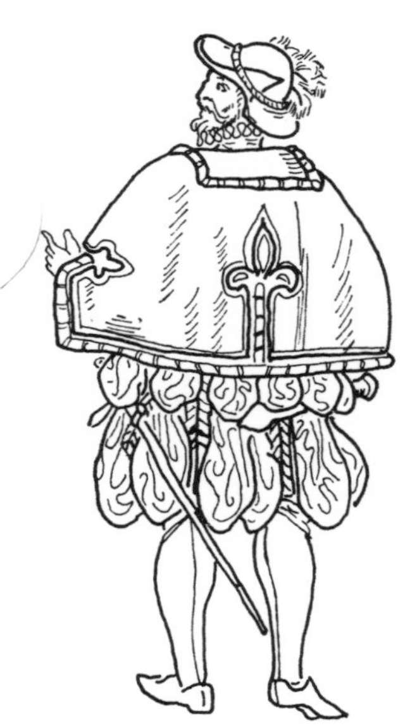

8. German. Short cloak known in Germany as the Spanish cape with "sailor" collar; pluderhose, silk inner linings extruding between panes and overhanging below knees. Second half 16th century. After *A History of Costume*, Carl Köhler.

The trunkhose, like the doublet, were generally distended by bombast, or by a combination of bombast and coarse underlinings of holland or canvas. There was also an outer lining of satin, taffeta, etc. An alternative means of distending the hose was by bearing them out with padded rolls around the waist or hips, or round the top of each leg.

Almost without exception trunks were decorated by " paning ". Panes were long vertical strips of material and could be obtained by slashing the material or by using separate strips joined only at top and bottom. Between the strips the lining was pulled out in " puffs " (Pl. 3). So universal was this decoration that trunkhose were sometimes known as " panes " or a " pair of panes ". In the extreme of this fashion were the German " pluderhose ". Of mainly German and Swiss military wear this form was sometimes affected by civilians at the end of the 16th century. " They were characterised by broad panes with wide gaps bulging with masses of silk or taffeta generally overhanging the panes below. These hose might be knee length or even longer " (Cunnington, *Handbook of English Costume in the 16th Century*) (Fig. 8).

The cod-piece (Fig. 9; Pls. 2 and 4). This addition to the front of the trunkhose first appeared in the mid 15th century when its purpose was to aid decency by covering the front gusset which was necessary in the tight hose of the time. As the situation eased, its original function was lost, and it remained as a cover to the front opening of the hose, and as an instance

9. Jerkin, sleeveless, pinked and paned, wings in pickadil, high-standing collar; small ruff; paned trunkhose with cod-piece. *c.* 1560–1565.
Don John of Austria (?). Alonso Sanchez Coelio.

10. Short "Dutch" breeches, open at knee; garter fringes visible; cuirass with sash or scarf over right shoulder; flat crowned tall hat. 1605.
King James I, engraving by Jan Wierax.

of male sexual vanity. In its last stages it was said to have been used as a handy pocket, much in the style of the Scotsman's sporran. By 1590 it had almost ceased to be worn, finally disappearing in the early 1600's.

Pockets of the usual type were set in the side seams of trunkhose.

Breeches proper. Three styles of breeches were in wear: first, Venetians (Figs. 4, 6 and 11) during the whole period 1570–1620, but most popular during the 1580's and 1590's, were of three designs, close fitting, pear shaped (wide at waist and narrow at the knee), or uniformly baggy throughout (these were, after 1610, pleated or gathered longitudinally): second, galligaskins or galligascoines or any one of a number of similar names. Despite modern research, doubt still remains as to the exact style and shape of these garments, but they seem to have resembled Venetians and were either close fitting or could be full in the seat. They were worn from about 1570 onwards.

The third style, open breeches or hose, were popular here from 1600 to 1610, and originated in Holland, where they were worn during the 1580's. They were open ended, like modern shorts, reaching just below the knee (Fig. 10). They sometimes had a slit at the sides to show the garters securing the stockings : when not slit the ends of the garter bow hung below the bottom of the legs.

Slops. Like galligaskins, this word is still of uncertain definition, being found in references to a variety of garments, but in the 16th and 17th centuries referring to some form of hose or breeches. In the earlier years of the 16th century the term seems to have been applied to the more exaggerated varieties of upper stocks ; later in that century, as in the 17th, to any wide baggy type of breeches, closed at the knee.

Just before the end of our period, in 1619, cloak-bag breeches were introduced. These were full, oval shaped, and gathered at the waist and knee.

In all types of separate breeches there were pockets, and a front vertical opening hidden by the folds of the material. Cod-pieces were not worn.

Stockings and garters. Nether stocks or nether stockings were terms often used for the separate stocking in the latter half of the 16th century. They were increasingly knitted, although some separate stockings were tailored from material cut on the cross. The tailored stocking had almost disappeared by 1600. The knitted variety were fashioned on a knitting frame from 1589 ; previously they had been hand-knitted. Wool was the commonest material; silk stockings were highly prized, and the last word in elegance : leather stockings have been noted. Clocks in the shape of wedges, point uppermost, of coloured silk, or gold and silver thread, embroidery were common as decoration, and the stockings could be brightly coloured.

Garters were either plain buckled straps, fastened below the knee with the stocking top rolled back over them, or ornamental bands or small sashes of material, ranging from worsted for the poor to gold, and jewel enriched silks for the rich man's leg (Figs. 5 and 11). Fringed ends of the garters were common, and can be seen dangling below the ends of open breeches, when the rest of the garter is concealed (Fig. 10). The tied garter was generally worn below the knee, with the bow on the outside of the leg: with canions and Venetians the stockings often came above the knee and the garter was tied there (Fig. 5).

From the 'sixties until about 1610 cross-gartering was fashionable to support stockings thus worn with canions: the garters were placed below

11. Richly embroidered jerkin, open to the waist; doublet with close-fitting sleeves; rigid, padded trunkhose with canions; stockings with garters with fringed ends. The boy in doublet and full Venetians, with a falling band. 1602.
Sir Walter Raleigh and his son. National Portrait Gallery, London.

12. Spanish. Jerkin over doublet with full sleeves; paned and padded trunkhose with canions; stockings cross-gartered; bonnet of medium height. *c.* 1570–80.
After *A History of Costume*. Carl Köhler.

the knee, the ends passed back and given a cross twist behind the knee and then brought forward again, this time above the knee, where they were tied in a bow, either in front or to one side (Fig. 12).

Boothose were originally coarse over-stockings, to protect finer ones from damage when boots were worn—for instance, when riding. Very occasionally they were worn with shoes. Later the boothose became ornamental, made of fine material, often embroidered at the top, or edged with lace. They could be fastened up to the breeches by decorative points.

THE JERKIN or JACKET. Whether or not Valentine honestly mistook Thurio's doublet for a jerkin[1] or was only pretending to, so as to " lead him up the garden " is immaterial. As the jerkin was almost identical in cut with the doublet, and followed its shape throughout the various changes of fashion, appearances might at times be deceptive. Generally worn over the doublet (by contemporary writers jerkins are classed with coats, cassocks and mandilions, while doublets are always referred to as in a category by themselves), it might, by the poor, be worn in place of it (Figs. 4, 5, 9 and 11).

It would appear that the jerkin, not being usually padded or busked, was often made of stout materials having a great deal of " body " ; leather and felt are examples. While these lent themselves especially to use in travel, hunting, or warfare, jerkins of superfine leather, handsomely embroidered, and perhaps perfumed, figured in courtly wear. The normal leather jerkin, often known as the *Buff jerkin*, was dressed ox-hide with a velvet-like surface : the body was often cut in panes from chest to waist ; the yoke and standing collar were either plain or pinked : the skirt, which was short, and occasionally double, might be paned also : it was usually scalloped or tabbed (pickadil).

Jerkins were also made in textile materials : velvet, satin, cloth of silver, russet, and frieze.

Skirts could be short, and variously shaped like the doublet skirts, or long, flaring over the trunk hose and covering the seat.

Sleeves were frequently absent, or if present might be long to the wrist, where they buttoned, or short, puffed-out shoulder sleeves. Alternatively hanging sleeves were fashionable with jerkins, either sham, being mere flat strips of material attached to the back of the armhole, or real hanging sleeves with open front seams, arranged to hang or else to fasten over the arm, wholly or in part, by buttons or points. Hanging sleeves, real or sham, might be worn with the short puff-sleeve. In the 1580's it was the done thing to have one hanging sleeve loose and wear the other.

Wings were always present in fashionable circles : certain " working " jerkins were sleeved with no wings.

While generally designed to open down the front, jerkins are sometimes found opening at the breast and up the sides. This latter would be put on over the head and a tight fit was secured by closely buttoning or hooking up the side opening. When opening down the whole of the front, fastenings

[1] *Two Gentlemen of Verona:* Act II, Sc. iv.

would be buttons, hooks and eyes, lacing, or a series of points. Often, however, the jerkin was worn partly or wholly open (Figs. 4 and 6).

Alternatively to slashing and pinking, jerkins might be decorated by embroidery or lace and braid trimming. Belts, when worn, were as for the doublet.

THE CLOAK was, throughout our period, the height of fashion, being worn more and more instead of the gown. As previously stated it was an essential part of one's apparel, worn indoors (but discarded when dancing) as well as out. The average length was to the fork, but from 1580 to 1620 the waist-length cloak or cape was very popular, and from the 1570's onwards a long ankle-length version was to be seen. All cloaks were voluminous, circular in plan, cut from three-quarters or more of a circle: some had small turned-down collars, some a standing collar, and some no collar at all, but with trimming up the sides and round the neck continuous with the trimming round the hem.

13. French cloak, worn over left shoulder. Late 16th century.
After *Handbook of English Costume in the 16th Century*. C. W. & P. E. Cunnington.

In the 17th century the cloak tended to match the doublet and breeches: the lining might correspond to that of the doublet, or be of velvet. A flat "sailor" collar appeared in the early 17th century also. A sleeved variety of cloak, becoming less popular after 1575, had either shoulder sleeves and hanging sleeves, or wrist-length close-hanging sleeves (Pl. 4). Such a cloak resembled very much a short gown.

Three popular named styles show how Continental fashions influenced English taste; these are the Spanish, French and Dutch cloaks.

The *Spanish* was a full short cloak or cape, which by 1560 was no more than waist length (Fig. 5). It had a small turned-down collar with a step to a turned-back border down to the hem. Its great distinguishing feature was a hood, which by our period was largely an ornamental feature only. The hood, together with the body of the cloak, was variously trimmed or "guarded", and the hood was lavishly bedecked with braid frogs or loops and buttons. The Spanish cloak stood out stiffly from the body, unlike the *French cloak,* which was long and not rigid, though full cut, circular or semicircular (Fig. 13). In length it was below the knees or even down to the ankles (a fashion held in disfavour by Gloriana, who is said to have forbidden anyone in her presence in a cloak of more than knee length). The French cloak often had an elbow-length shoulder cape. The usual mode of wearing was draped over the left shoulder, and it was difficult to keep on. Guards, braid, lace and embroidery, and even beads, pearls and gems adorned the French cloak. Elaborate guarding was also characteristic of the *Dutch cloak,* another full, short variety, but in this case with wide sleeves.

14. Cloak, showing method of securing. 1605. From a contemporary print of the Gunpowder Plot Conspirators.

The method of securing the cloak seems in general to have been by cords, with tassels of gold, silver or silk, attached to the lining at the neck. When the cloak was worn over both shoulders the cords were passed under the arms backwards and tied between the shoulder blades, underneath the cloak of course. From the 1560's it was popular to wear the cloak over one shoulder : in this case the cords were passed back under the opposite armpit and were tied behind, or around the arm itself, in either case out of sight, later they passed round the neck and tied in a bow at the back (Fig. 14). The fullness of the cloak in front was often caught up in the hand or held up under the elbow (Fig. 13).

All types of cloaks could be made from a wide variety of silks, velvets and less expensive stuffs. Colours were as varied : white, red, tawny, black, green, russet, purple, violet, etc. Sleeved varieties of cloak were commonly black. Linings might be as rich as the outer material : fur was used both as a trimming and for lining. Some cloaks had back or side vents, usually guarded ; these cloaks were originally for wear when riding.

Short cloaks, though always worn to some extent, tended to become rarer towards the end of our period, and the Spanish and Dutch styles were much more fashionable in the 16th than in the 17th century.

PLATE 3

Black and white armour : gorget or collar, cuirass, tasses, pauldrons, and vambraces. Slight peascod-belly to cuirass. Short trunkhose. Slashed shoes with pickadils round foot. *c.* 1585.

Philip II of Spain : attrib. to S. Anguisciol.
National Portrait Gallery, London.

THE GOWN (Fig. 15). This once universal garment became less worn as the cloak increased in popularity, and by 1600 it had become almost entirely restricted to State officials, the learned professions and to the elderly as formal dress. Knee-length gowns lingered on into the very beginning of our period, but the majority of gowns between 1570 and 1600 were to the ankle. Respectable townsmen of the merchant class were apt to walk abroad in their gowns, which were either worn open in front or caught in at the waist by a belt or narrow sash knotted in front: it was also worn by older men in the home for ease and warmth or as a négligé, and when so used it was often termed a "night gown". It was ornamented with guards of bands of velvet or other material and often had a fur lining or trimming. Collars might be a square "sailor" with broad revers continuing as a turned-back edge to the bottom of the gown, or a stand collar with a step and narrow turned-back edge. Sleeves were long, tubular, with an upper opening for the arms, when they were worn as hanging sleeves, or puffed shoulder sleeves only, gathered into a band, and with sham hanging sleeves, often no more than a strip of material. The gown itself fell in folds from a fitted yoke. The common materials for making a gown were cloth, satin and velvet. The essentials of this garment are preserved today in the robes of Mayors, the Lord Chancellor and similar civil dignatories.

15. Citizen of London. Flat cap; fur-lined gown with hanging sleeves. 1572.
Engraving from *Civitates Orbis Terrarum*. Braun & Hogenburg.

With both cloak and gown could be worn a "tippet", which was a short shoulder cape, commonly of velvet or silk.

OTHER OVER-GARMENTS to be met with were the cassock, the mandilion and the gaberdine. Of these the *cassock* was, at this time, a straight, loose jacket to the hips, or just below, widening towards the hem (Fig. 16). It, again, was mostly a middle-class garment, but elaborate versions of costly stuffs were also to be seen. It had a low stand collar and full sleeves—either short above the elbow, or wrist-length. It was sometimes worn beneath the gown for extra warmth.

The mandilion was most common in the 1580's, but continued in general wear up to 1620, after which date it was restricted to livery only. This is in a way a reversion to its original status as a specialized garment, as it started its career as a military habit. It was, during the period *c.* 1580–1620, a hip-length garment, loose in cut, with the side seams left open. It had a stand

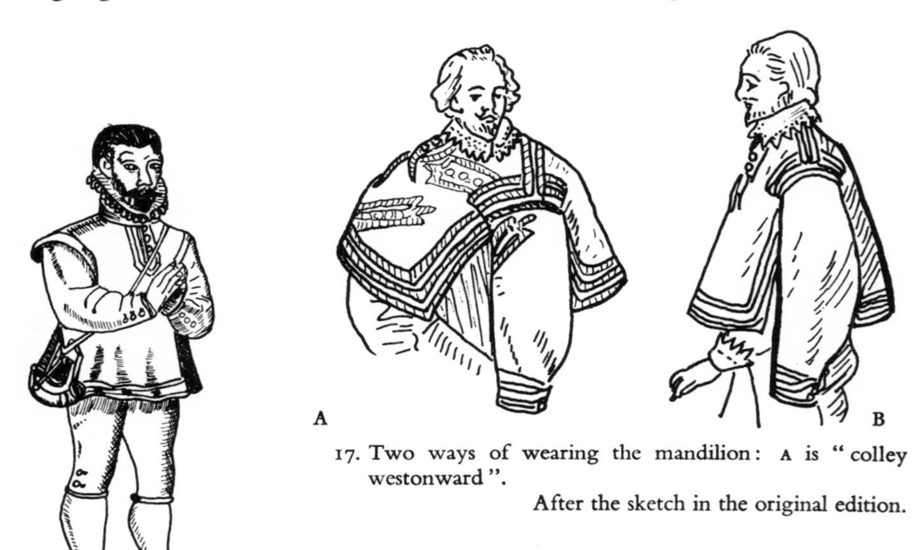

17. Two ways of wearing the mandilion: A is "colley westonward".
After the sketch in the original edition.

16. Countryman in cassock and tight Venetians. 1587.
Brass in Walton-on-Thames Church.

collar and hanging sleeves; in its later stages these were false. In front it had an opening, secured by buttons, from collar to chest, and it was put on over the head (Fig. 17b). It was frequently worn sideways, i.e. with the front and back hanging down over the arms and the sleeves dangling fore and aft. This method of wearing was known as "to Colley-weston ward", "Colley weston" being a Cheshire expression for anything gone wrong (Fig. 17a).

The gaberdine, a long, loose, wide-sleeved overcoat, was worn by men and women of all classes: made in felt, it was worn as a raincoat. Perhaps akin to it was the riding coat, with or without a hood, mentioned in the early years of the 17th century. The *chammer* or *shamew* is also to be met with. This appears to have been a gown-like loose coat, worn open and often of rich material, perhaps trimmed with fur.

The word "coat" appears to have been applied generally to upper garments such as the jerkin, mandilion, cassock, gaberdine and, occasionally, the gown, but never to the doublet. (A *base-coat* was a plain jerkin with skirts made longer than usual, and was also largely a military and livery garment.) To quote a contemporary moralist:

> "their coats and jerkins as they be diverse in colors, so be they diverse in fashions, for some be made with colars, some without; some close to the bodie, some loose, which they call mandilions covering the whole body down to the thighe, like bagges or sacks . . . some are buttoned downe the breast, some under the arme, and some down the back; some with flappes over the brest, some without; some with great sleeves, some with small, and some with non at all; some pleated and crested behind and curiouslye gathered, and some not so."[1]

A complexity of garments and styles which today is difficult to describe in all its varied details; indeed, even Stubbs himself talks of the mandilion as thigh length, which seems from contemporary pictures not to be the case.

UNDERCLOTHES. Under this heading I include the *waistcoat* which was a waist-length under-doublet, padded and usually quilted and with or without sleeves. Towards the end of the 16th century some apparently had a neck opening and side fastenings, and were put on over the head. Primarily worn for warmth, it was also sometimes an object of show as when the waistcoat was worn as a négligé, minus the doublet. Its older name, at this period rapidly becoming obsolete, was "petticoat". It was also known from about 1600 as a "vest", a term still used by tailors for a waistcoat.

Shirts were usually of cambric or holland and, from the middle of our period, lawn and silk. Countrymen and workmen generally probably made do with a tough canvas.

The finer varieties of shirt were often embroidered and lace edged, and had a "falling band" or turn down collar, or else a goffered collar, or ruff. Wrists were decorated by frills or "ruffles" or turned back cuffs. The cut of the Elizabethan shirt was much the same as those of today, but somewhat

[1] Stubbs, *Anatomie of Abuses*, 1585 (3rd Edn.).

fuller. There were generally two side slits or vents producing the characteristic shirt tails, and the neck opening was just sufficient to pull the shirt over the head.

The falling band was spread out over the doublet collar in the 1570's to 1590's, and was often bordered with lace (Fig. 18 ; Pl. 1). Falling bands varied in size, cut and decoration during the period up to 1620, and after 1585 they became a separate article from the shirt. Early in the 17th century the standing band or "Golilla" was introduced. This was a semicircular collar, the curved outer edge standing up around the back of the neck and head and the straight-cut front edges tied under the chin with bandstrings (Pl. 5). The stand-up portion was supported by a wire frame attached to the neck of the doublet and known as a "supportasse", "underpropper" or "rebato" (Fig. 36). Occasionally this standing band was worn without the rear support, and turned down over the shoulders in the manner of a falling band. Falling and standing bands had, after the separation from the shirt, deep neckbands of their own.

18. Falling bands; four, one over the other, the top one lace-edged: gorget; spade beard. *c.* 1590.
Sir Peter Eure. After the sketch in the original edition.

The ruff, like the bands or collars, had a fairly deep neckband after its separation from the shirt. The ruff evolved from a frilly edging to the shirt neckband, which by 1570 had so increased in size as to become an article of dress in its own right. In the 1580's it reached immense size, decreasing again after about 1610, dying out about the end of our period. Ruffs were originally single goffered bands (Pl. 2), but during the years approximately 1580–1620 they were often of compound construction containing two, three or more layers of material (Fig. 5). The goffering into tubular pleats called "sets" was carried out by setting-sticks, also known as poking-sticks or pokers: they were of bone, ivory, wood or metal, and when heated were applied to the starched material of the ruff to produce the familiar radiating organ-pleats, often as horizontal or vertical figures-of-eight.

The very large "cartwheel" ruffs were, like standing bands, supported at the back by the supportasse or underpropper, or by means of a "pickadil".

This last, deriving its name from the tabbed decoration of the period, was an upright stiffened frame, edged with tabs turned out horizontally, and fixed to the back of the doublet at the neck. The fashionable forward tilt of the large ruffs was also aided by the cut of the doublet collar, sloping to the front.

Bands and ruffs were generally of linen ; but sometimes also of cambric, holland, lawn, lace or lockeram (a coarse linen favoured by poorer people). In the 16th century bands were sometimes embroidered in silk or metal thread, or decorated with cut-and-drawn work. Ruffs were similarly treated, in their case lasting into the 17th century. Lace was also used as an edging or insertion—one of the characteristics of the 17th century is the profuse use of lace by both sexes.

A variation seen during the last few years of our period was the falling ruff, made of several layers of material, gathered into a high neckband without formal setting, and worn drooping down on to the shoulders.

Both ruffs and bands were starched from the introduction of starch into England some time in the 1560's. Sometimes coloured starch was used, generally yellow, but in contemporary pictures the commonest colour for neckwear is white.

Sometimes a ruff and a falling band were worn together, the ruff on top.

Bands and ruffs alike were secured under the chin by band-strings which tied the ends together, either, as was most general, completely closed around the neck throughout the width, or with a V-shaped gap at the front. The ruff in particular was generally worn, especially by men, closed all round : the variety of design in the falling band allowed of a greater choice in the matter. The band-strings were most often concealed, but sometimes the tasselled end might be left visible (Pl. 5).

Cuffs, turned back over the doublet sleeve and trimmed to match the neckwear, were worn with falling and standing bands, and occasionally with ruffs (Pls. 1 and 5). Ruffles, or hand-ruffs, were like mini neck-ruffs and worn with them, never with bands (Pls. 3 and 4). Both cuffs and ruffles were in origin part of the shirt sleeve. In the late 16th and up to mid 17th century the cuff was a separate article, attached to the shirt wrist. The ruffle was generally in one with the shirt, but detachable ruffles were also known.

The embroidery or other decoration of the bands, cuffs, etc., could also be repeated at the bottom hem and at the side vents of the shirt.

Drawers, sometimes called "strossers" or "trousers", or variants of these two words, were the equivalent of the modern pants. They were generally of linen, so cut to fit tightly. They might be of knee or ankle length; later in the 17th century very short square-cut drawers, fuller than the earlier styles, were introduced. These latter might be of silk. For practical stage purposes today ordinary short pants will suffice.

Half shirt. This was a short undershirt, worn for warmth and noted in Scotland in 1578: English references are later. From some descriptions it appears that the half shirt was often decorated with lace, and an alternative mode of wearing it was possibly over the shirt proper, where its profusion of lace would not blush unseen.

Night shirts appear to have been much the same as the day shirts—probably plainer at this time, though later in the 17th century night shirts were every bit as elaborate as day.

Night caps (see also page 42) were of quilted cotton, or fustian interlined with wool or flock: fine specimens would be of velvet. Red was a favourite colour.

FOOTWEAR. Shoes were low heeled, except for a type of cork wedge which came in about 1595, until the beginning of the 17th century, when raised heels became popular. Heels were generally of leather or wood. Cork was also sometimes used to thicken the soles from about 1595. During our period the toes of both shoes and boots were rounded or bluntly pointed.

The shoe of this period was close-fitting and covered the whole foot. Till after 1570 the upper was made (vamp and quarter) of the one piece, and, having no fastening, required the use of a shoe-horn. Apart from material and colour, among the better classes the great majority of shoes were almost identical in cut and decoration till about 1570 (Fig. 19a). From that date on, vamp and quarter are cut separately. The former has the upper edge (tongue) either arched or with a blunt point; the latter is prolonged in front on either side in a couple of broad thongs or ankle-straps meeting over the instep where they are secured by a *point* passing through eyelet-holes (Fig. 19c). Sometimes these straps are tied over the vamp sometimes under it (out of sight). More rarely the vamp also has a pair of eyelets in the tongue and the ties, passing through these also, are fastened on the outside. From the 'eighties onward we find a gradually increasing tendency to leave an opening over the ankle on either side between vamp and quarter; a fashion general and ever more marked from *c.* 1600. Soon after this we first meet *shoe-roses* (Fig. 19d) (= shoe rosettes) masking the fastening, side by side with large ribbon-bows (Fig. 19e). Another new fashion of the early 1600's was that of dyeing the heels and edges of the soles red for wear with full dress.

Pantoffles. These were slipper-like overshoes with extra-thick cork soles. Some were of stout leather and had the soles set with iron: these were to keep the feet out of the mire. But, as so often happens at this date, there were others of a luxurious character, mainly of black velvet. These were used even in company and consisted of a mere vamp (often hardly more

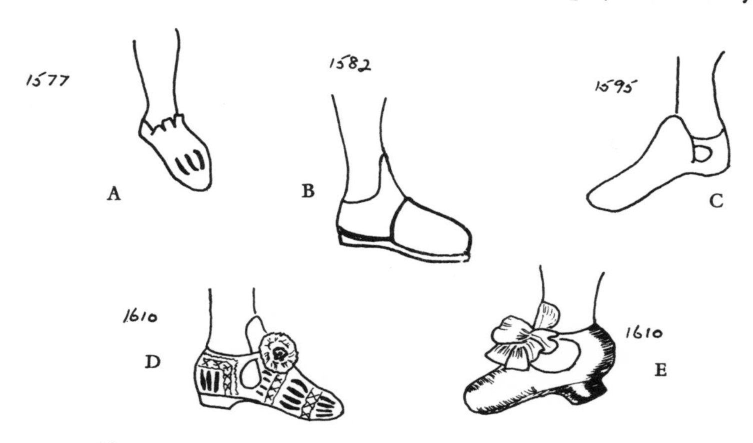

19. Shoes. In B *pantoffles* are worn over the high-tongued shoe.
From various portraits.

than a toe-cap) set upon a sole that thickened, wedge-like, from toe to heel, where it might be two inches or so high (Fig. 19b). How they were kept on is generally a moot point, although in rare instances one sees a *point* on the toe-cap, presumably serving that purpose. The thickening of the sole doubtless recommended them to such as were tempted to add to their apparent stature. Another variety of protective overshoes, or galoshes, was the patten, which had a wooden or thick leather sole, and strapped over the shoes.

Boots or Buskins. Except for travelling, hunting, by soldiers serving on horseback and the like, boots were no very common feature of Elizabethan costume until after *c.* 1585; towards 1610 boots and spurs sprang into rapidly increasing favour, being not excluded from the drawing-room. As worn by soldiers and sportsmen, the Elizabethan boots are usually tall, and made of soft, stretchable leather, reaching well above the knee (beneath which they can be turned down and folded *ad lib.*) and often slit down at the back to facilitate flexion of the limb. Among the better classes they are shaped to the limb. There were also shorter kinds : buskins to the knee or even to mid-leg only. To ensure a close fit over the small of the leg they may be slit down and laced or buttoned together or tightened with straps and buckles on the outer side. An alternate device is to decorate the boot with a pinked design which causes the leather to " give " and facilitates pulling on and off. Boots were self-coloured or black, and usually kept in supple condition when not in use by a liberal coating of grease.

Particularly in Spain the boots were often braced up to the trunkhose in front by means of a Λ-shaped strap.

The tops of the boots were often " wrought in pickadils "or scalloped, and might be faced with velvet.

The countryman wore rough leather ankle boots known as " startups ", or " cockers ", which were high laced boots at this time.

There was also—although this is perhaps commoner in Spain and Italy—a variety of boots of a definitely " dressy " kind. These are made of fine Spanish leather, mostly white or biscuit-coloured. They were often *en suite* with the fine jerkins of perfumed Spanish leather and their natural pliancy was enhanced by decorative pinking, or even slashing.

In *16th-century costumes*, however, these dress boots should be used sparingly.

HEADWEAR. Hats or bonnets were, as previously stated, always retained indoors on formal occasions, during certain dances, and at meals. When the hat was removed undercaps were often disclosed and kept on the head, even in the presence of the Monarch. The custom of raising the hat or cap in greeting was established by the latter years of the 16th century, during which period the height of all forms of headwear began to increase so that by 1600 tall crowned hats and caps were *le dernier cri*.

The buttoned cap and flat cap were two earlier styles which retained a low brow popularity : after 1570 the flat cap (Fig. 15) tended to be restricted to citizens, apprentices and artisans of London. In 1571 the Statute Cap was introduced by Act of Parliament. It was of knitted wool and was to be worn on Sundays and holy-days by all except the nobility and " other persons of degree ", in a pious effort to boost the wool trade. The Act was repealed in 1597.

Bonnets with low or tall bag-like crowns were worn perched or tilted over one eye (Figs. 20 and 21) and vied in popular esteem with innumerable

20. Bonnets: jewelled bands and plumes.
From portraits of Sir Christopher Hatton (A) and the Earl of Oxford (B). *c.* 1580 and 1575.

varieties of hat, high (most popular) or low, round, or flat topped, made of beaver, felt, silk, velvet, fur, leather and a number of other less popular materials (Figs. 11 and 22). There was a wide selection of headgear which

21. Bonnet with medium-height pleated crown, jewelled band and plume. *c.* 1572.
Charles IX of France. François Clouet.

22. Flat-topped, medium-height hat with decorated band, jewels, and plume. Multiple ruff. 1603.
King James I. Lawrence Johnson.

tended to become more restricted with the advance of the 17th century, when the cap became decidely unfashionable and the hats settled down into wide brimmed, flat or conical crowned, shapes.

During our period up to 1610, or thereabouts, the copotain hat was very fashionable (Fig. 4). This had a high crown of conical shape (later in the 17th century the name "sugar-loaf" was applied to a revival of the copotain), with a moderate width flat brim, which might be rolled or with a moderate turn up, or cock. In the last quarter of the 16th century another popular shape was not unlike a modern "bowler" (Fig. 23).

Monmouth caps, brimless, with tall crowns, were favoured by Welshmen, soldiers and sailors; which last also wore the "thrummed" hat, wool or silk woven hats with a shaggy nap or pile. Thrummed hats were also worn by the labouring classes at this period.

23. Hat with "Bowler"-shaped crown, high-necked doublet; falling band; Marquisetto beard. 1570's. Antoine de la Mark. *Bibliothèque Nationale, Paris.*

Hats, bonnets and caps were all more or less elaborately trimmed with bands, feathers, pinked patterns, and even, among the wealthy, jewels.

Elegant *night caps* were worn indoors, usually with the night gown, which corresponded to the modern dressing-gown or smoking-jacket. Night caps had a closely turned-up brim and a deep crown and were made of embroidered silk, cloth, or linen, brocade or velvet (Pl. 5).

Coifs, close fitting white linen caps tied under the chin, were worn by the learned professions, under a hat or cap or alone (Fig. 24). Black coifs were sometimes worn by the elderly for warmth, as were black skull caps

HAIR. Right through the period we meet with fairly close-cropped hair in all classes of society, but in course of time other modes enjoyed a more or less widespread vogue, especially among younger men. The close crop was universal throughout the 'sixties. It may have been Don John of Austria's resounding victory of Lepanto in 1571—he was a "glass of fashion and mould of form"—that popularized his way of dressing the hair off the forehead in an upright bush. From this rapidly developed a new style in which the hair over the crown and at the sides stood upright "like a swine's bristles", being stiffened with gum. Those who had naturally curly locks allowed them to grow in a full crop all over the pate. By the 'nineties there is a notable inclination to flowing locks—formerly the nape had been "shingled" (Fig. 24)—though it but rarely (e.g. in the case of George Clifford, Earl of Cumberland) attempts to rival the luxuriance of the " Cavalier " period. Note that the hair is consistently trained *off the forehead.* The *love-lock* (mentioned as far back as 1592) was a long lock allowed to grow at the side, where it hung down in a free tress or narrow plait, sometimes decked with ribbons, to the breast.

Down to 1577 there were still a number of conservative old men who went clean-shaven, although otherwise from the beginning of this period practically everybody was more or less bearded. *Per contra* many of the older folk sported beards worthy of a Hebrew prophet. The commonest form of beard with all classes was of moderate length, more or less pointed, with close-cropped whiskers. But from the 'eighties on we meet with many other varieties. Though a number of these are known to us by name, it is a very different matter to recognize them all at sight. However we may with fair probability identify the following types.

24. Lawyer wearing a white coif; gown and hood. *c.* 1585.
Detail of a painting of the Court of Wards and Liveries. *Goodwood Collection.*

The *pickedevant* seems to have been short and pointed, worn with a brushed-up moustache (Fig. 16).

The " forked " or " swallow-tail " cut explains itself.

The " stiletto " beard was presumably an imperial, cut to a sharp point.

The *marquisetto* was cropped fairly close (but irregularly) hardly masking the contour of the chin. It suggests a very imperfect shave (Fig. 23).

The " spade " beard appears to have been square cut.

The tendency as time went on was for the whiskers to shrink and eventually vanish sometime in the 1590's.

The moustache on an otherwise shaven face is extremely rare before the Civil Wars outside central and eastern Europe. It is hardly seen in the south and west except as an immature growth on quite young men. As worn with the beard, it was at first allowed to follow its natural direction ; from the 'seventies the tendency is to train it stiffly upward.

GIRDLE, SWORD and DAGGER. The girdle throughout this era was a narrow strap fastened with a clasp in front. As we have seen, it followed the direction of the waist-line of doublet and jerkin, and so in most cases sinks in a deep V over the abdomen. For the purpose of carrying a sword it was mounted with sliding buckles ending in rings for the attachment of a pair of *hangers*. These will be best understood by reference to illustrations (Fig. 25a). Both hangers and the girdle for their support were generally of leather, more or less ornamented ; alternatively fabric could be used,

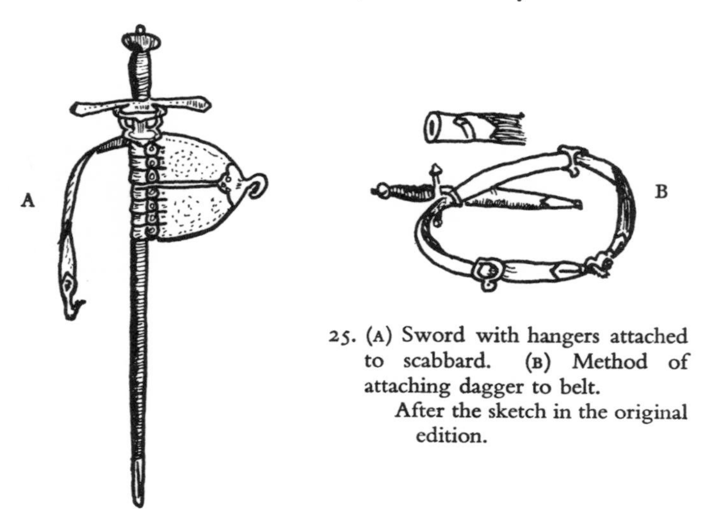

25. (A) Sword with hangers attached to scabbard. (B) Method of attaching dagger to belt.
After the sketch in the original edition.

on a leather foundation. By unhooking the hangers the sheathed sword could be discarded without removing the belt (Fig. 25). The girdle may be worn *ad lib.* next the doublet or over the jerkin.

The sheath of the sword was thrust through the loops at the base of the hangers which could be tightened or relaxed by adjusting the buckles. By shifting the sliding buckles back or forward on the belt the hang of the sword could be regulated to taste. The side-piece of the hangers might be threaded through the *panes*. Note that, when thrust home in the scabbard, sword and dagger fitted sufficiently tightly to require a definite tug to release them. Thus, even when worn horizontally, there was little risk of their being casually dislodged and lost. The dagger was worn on the right hip or, more often, above the right buttock. It could be slung from a short chain or tied to the belt by a cord. The most typical attachment, however, was that shown (Fig. 25b) : by means of a small staple affixed to the locket of the sheath which could thus be threaded on the girdle. The staple was shaped like a / a \ or a ×, the last type allowing the dagger to hang horizontally with the hilt turned to right or left at choice.

SCARVES and SASHES of silk began to be worn from about 1580; for warmth round the neck, for show draped over one shoulder or round the waist. Worn with the buff coat or leather jerkin it was the mark of the military and quasi-military man. Scarves were sometimes elaborately embroidered and often edged with gold lace (Fig. 10).

GORGETS, or steel collars, vestigial armour, were also worn by manly young (and not so young) civilians during the period under review (Pl. 2).

GLOVES. The familiar "gauntlet" type with huge fringed and embroidered cuffs hardly appears till the closing years of the 16th century. Stout, plain leather gauntlets were used for sport.

The typical 16th-century glove among the well-dressed has a short cuff, with a border of looped pickadils or tabs and decorated with purely ornamental points. The hand portion was of thin leather, slightly decorated; the cuff of leather or velvet, usually contrasting in colour. These gloves were *carried* in token of gentility rather than worn, and might be stuck through the girdle. Rarely were both worn at once.

Perfumed gloves were imported from France and Spain.

WALKING-CANES were rather tall, with—often very handsomely—wrought metal knobs. Native woods were among the wealthy giving place to exotic growths. Canes were used mostly by the old or infirm.

RIDING-CANES were lithe rods commonly made of holly, often quite plain and unmounted.

HANDKERCHIEFS were usually made of linen, lawn or cambric and elaborate ones were decorated with tassels or buttons at the corners, cut work, embroidery in blue thread or silk and gold thread, and lace edges. Silk was also used to make handkerchiefs and velvet ones were imported from Italy. These were all for show rather than blow and were carried in the hand or girdle or protruded from the doublet sleeve. Plain linen squares served as practical handkerchiefs.

Occasionally *masks* to conceal identity, and, from 1600, *muffs* to warm the hands were used by men, although they were more essentially feminine accessories.

JEWELLERY. Apart from collars of office, knightly orders and kindred insignia, jewellery was pretty freely displayed at this date, particularly in the second half of the period. Not only does it take the form of necklaces, bracelets, ear-rings, finger rings and pendants, but the more ostentatious courtiers actually wore gems, pearls and goldsmith's work as trimmings to their clothes. Buttons, clasps, brooches and aglets were often of a showy kind, whether used as fastenings or mere decoration; though it should be borne in mind that much of this was sham. Lockets and miniatures were commonly worn. Both Queen Elizabeth and James I encouraged their favourites to make a brave show at court: Leicester, Hatton, Raleigh and Oxford were at least rivalled in this respect by Somerset and Buckingham.

CHAPTER III

WOMEN'S CLOTHES, 1570-1620

I would wish, Mistress Raffaella, to hear somewhat more of you in the matter of dress.
Piccolomini, 1538.

As in men's apparel, so also in women's the fashionable ideal was a wooden rigidity of outline, emphasized by busks and padding, wide hips and puffed-up shoulders contrasting with the wasp-waist. At first the female form seems modelled on an hour-glass ; then the strangled torso appears to emerge from a big drum. The merciless tight-lacing forces the breasts upward and outward above the bodice, thereby exaggerating the wearers' feminity.

VERDINGALE (or *farthingale*). The woman of this era is so identified with her *verdingale* that for once this may be given pride of place in the enumeration of her wardrobe. In its earlier form the verdingale originated in Spain, the name being ultimately derived from Spanish *verdugo,* a flexible rod. It was an under-petticoat, distended by a series of hoops of cane, wire, etc., their compass increasing progressively downward. Occasionally it has but a single hoop : at the hem. The effect in most cases is to eliminate all folds and to lend to the wearer, from the waist downward, the shape of an extinguisher. This is the original or so-called "Spanish" verdingale (Figs. 26 and 28a). In Spain and those districts that followed her fashions the type persisted well into the 17th century. Sometimes in its later forms it fetched an exaggerated compass at the hem. The "French", either wheel or roll, variety began to compete with it in the west soon after 1575 and eventually superseded it in France, England and the Netherlands. In this the maximum girth started immediately at the hips and the skirts hung vertically from there to the ground (Fig. 27). This might be achieved by a hoop-like framework, but more commonly by a thick padded roll, known with true Elizabethan directness as a "bum-roll", tied about the waist and resembling a motor tyre or lifebuoy (Fig. 28b). It had a forward tilt, causing it to ride up behind. The "semi-circled farthingale" was a half-roll at the back, leaving the front flat. By the last few years of the

16th century the horizontal set of the skirt at the hips was accentuated by a circular flounce or *frounce* of the same material as the skirt, gathered into radiating, ruff-like pleats and resting flat on the top of the farthingale (Fig. 27). To avoid the indiscreet revelations that might follow an awkward

26. Spanish farthingale skirt. In this instance the skirt is arranged in even folds from the waist. Hanging sleeves, ruff and cuffs. Small muff. *c.* 1580.
Countess of Oxford & Elgin.
National Trust.

27. French farthingale skirt with frounce; very low bodice, fashionable in the early 17th century, sleeves with wings and sham hanging sleeves. Standing band at back of head, deep cuffs. Feather fan. *c.* 1610.
Queen Anne, wife of James I.
Paul van Somer.

fall, it was found expedient beneath both types of farthingales to wear under-petticoats. In Italy, knickers were worn during the years under review, but these immodest garments did not cross the Channel for another two centuries or more.

BODICE. From mid-century and until about 1625 women's dresses were generally made as separate bodices and skirts. The one-piece gown of earlier times persisted in some cases, worn over the bodice and skirt or over a skirt only. Like the men's doublets the bodice sank to a more or

PLATE 4

Doublet with high stand collar ; ruff and ruffles edged with lace ; full trunkhose, paned, with cod-piece ; cassock ; small (court) bonnet with ostrich feather and jewelled decoration to match cassock sleeves. 1560's.

Earl of Leicester (or Suffolk ?) : unknown artist.
National Portrait Gallery, London.

less acute point in front. The slightly arched décolletage of the Holbein era persists till the 'seventies. In Italy the bosom is generally more or less exposed. In England and the Netherlands the tendency is to fill up the décolletage by a high-necked chemise or an embroidered partlet (Pl. 6). In France both these fashions were in vogue. The Spanish fashion was for a bodice closed high up to the neck, and this style also had its partisans in the other countries, side-by-side with those already described. Bodices or "pairs of bodies", were stiffened in a corset-like manner with busks of wood or whalebone. Similarly stiffened under-bodices, sometimes of leather, were an alternative, and a precursor of true corsets. Generally speaking, however, the stiffened bodice, integral with the dress, was the rule during this period. Up to 1580, the ladies' bodice, like the male doublet, might be freely garnished with pickadils, which often formed a short skirt below the pointed waist.

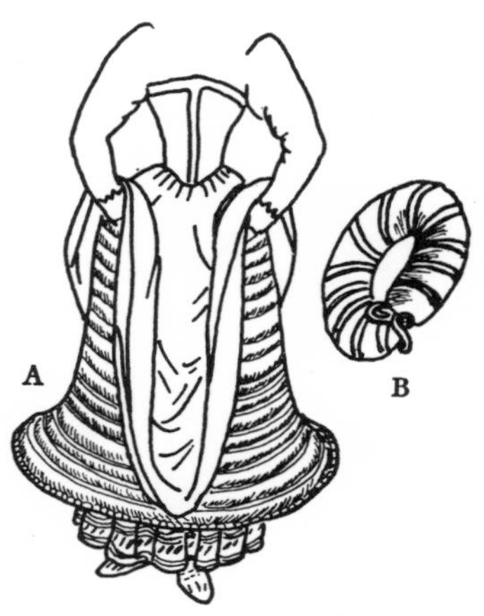

28. (A) Spanish farthingale exposed; note under-petticoat. (B) Bum-roll form of French farthingale.
(A) Print of *c.* 1575. (B) Dutch print of 1590.

Short pointed bodices (Pl. 6) might have high or low necks, the former with stand collars, or a variety of Medici collar. With the stand collar a cartwheel ruff was popular from the 'seventies, in which case the bodice was buttoned or hooked together at the front; otherwise a hooked fastening at the left-hand side was usual.

Sleeves were close fitting to the wrist, and were more or less padded. They might be slashed and puffed, or slit down the front to expose the chemise sleeve, and generally had wings. A very full puffed-out sleeve, ending with a deep cuff above the elbow, with a possibly detachable tight, wrist-length undersleeve was a variety, as was the "bishop" sleeve, full to the wrist and there tight with a cuff.

Hanging sleeves, sometimes false, were worn also, usually matching the dress, while the true sleeve teamed with the forepart.

In about 1580 long pointed bodices appeared. These had low necks and were often worn with a stomacher (Fig. 29), a triangular, stiffened centre to the bodice to which it was tied or pinned at each side. Stomachers often contrasted in colour and material with the bodice itself, but matched the sleeves and/or forepart of the skirt. An alternative mode for wear with the wheel farthingale was the round, or Dutch, waist.

With the long pointed bodice bombasted " bishop " sleeves were worn for about ten years from *c.* 1575, and until 1620 sleeves tapering from a full " kick up " at the shoulder to close fitting at the wrist, rigidly stuffed out with buckram, whalebone, etc., were known as " trunk " or " cannon " sleeves (Fig. 29). These sleeves could be ornamented with slashes or pinking, lace or embroidery, and had wings, rolls, or long false hanging sleeves in addition.

29. French farthingale skirt with frounce. Bodice with square neckline, long stomacher front and trunk sleeves. Very large hanging sleeves behind. Lace ruff and wired, jewelled head-rail. Jewelled ornament and pearls in hair. Fan and gloves 1592.
Queen Elizabeth I. Unknown artist. National Portrait Gallery.

The décolletage of the bodice from the last quarter of the 16th century alters its outline. The opening had been arched ; it was now mostly rounded, oval or V-shaped. Towards 1610 the décolletage was at times so deep as entirely to discover the breasts. Under Elizabeth to expose the bosom (in moderation) had been a token of maidenhood and as such affected by Queen Elizabeth in her latter years.

In the 17th century a jacket, often of linen, embroidered, was worn with a loose skirt *sans* farthingale. The jacket was an easy alternative to the bodice proper, not busked, often quilted for warmth. Sleeves were tight, and the waistline was straight with a small flared skirt (Pl. 7). The jacket seems to have gone out of fashion shortly after the end of our period. The exact difference from a *waistcoat* (q.v.) is difficult to determine.

Cloaks, or capes, were generally long and used as travelling garments, as was the safeguard, or overskirt, and the lap mantle, or rug. Cassocks appear to have been like the men's, sometimes with a hood, with loose open sleeves. Probably akin, but shorter, was the coat, which cannot with certainty be identified.

Dresses, gowns and cloaks were made from a wide range of materials ; by the wealthy classes no expense was spared and taffeta, silk, velvet, etc., vied with the humbler textiles such as linen, buckram, say, and varieties of cloth.

Lavish decoration in the form of embroidery, ribbons, lace, braid, guards of velvet, fringes, etc., often enriched with pearls and jewels, added to the splendour of the rich silks and damasks of the Court ladies.

SKIRT (*or KIRTLE*). The outline of the skirt is usually governed by the underlying verdingale, the acme of *chic* being to eliminate as far as possible all casual creases. Where no verdingale is worn, its place is taken by several full petticoats of stiff material and the skirt, gathered on the hips, falls in a few broad, tubular folds. The skirt and petticoat throughout the 16th century barely cleared the ground. Trains were only worn by great ladies and on state occasions. After 1600 the skirts of young women are often curtailed almost to ankle length.

The skirt could be closed in front or open in a ∧ to reveal the contrasting petticoat or forepart.

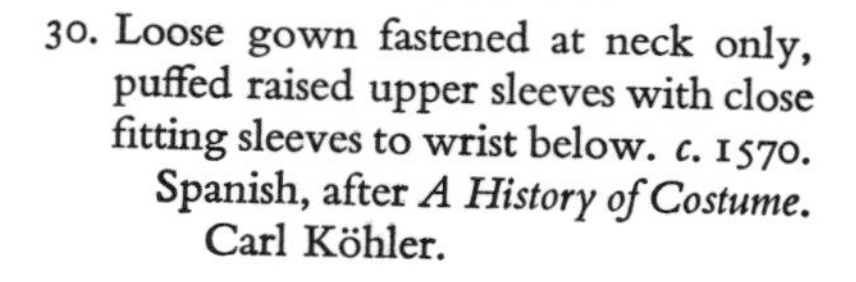

30. Loose gown fastened at neck only, puffed raised upper sleeves with close fitting sleeves to wrist below. *c.* 1570. Spanish, after *A History of Costume.* Carl Köhler.

GOWNS. Women's gowns were much in evidence for warmth and on "full dress" occasions, and, like the "Spanish" verdingale, attained their maximum fullness at the hem. There are two basic forms:

1. In this the gown, fitted to the shoulders, hangs from thence almost in the form of a bell-tent (Fig. 30).

2. The upper part is artfully cut so that, when buttoned to the waist, it has all the effect of a shaped bodice, the skirt being gathered on to it and spreading downward in funnel form (Fig. 31).

The "loose gown" was usually left open or buttoned at the throat only whence it opened downward in a great ∧, disclosing the underlying bodice and skirt. The second type of gown could also be worn open from throat to hem, but lent itself less readily to the process. There were also gowns with a deep, button-up slash down either breast to the waist, whereby the upper portion of the gown could be tightened to the figure (Fig. 31).

These gowns, almost to the close of the 16th century, mostly had short sleeves to the elbow swelling at the top into tall puffs that towered above the shoulders (Fig. 30). They are equipped with tall upright collars, which are a conspicuous feature when the gown is worn completely open, as they then take a marked outward curve. Flat or round turned-down collars were also seen. The wide shoulder-puffs were ostensibly designed to cover the high, padded wings of the bodice underneath. Beneath the puffs were tight undersleeves. Sometimes sleeveless gowns, or gowns with wings and hanging sleeves, were alternatives. The gown is usually adorned with broad guards of braid or dark velvet and with a plethora of buttons and loops serving both as a decoration and as fastenings.

31. Fitted gown fastened to waist, puffed shoulder sleeves continuing close fitting to wrist, sham hanging sleeves; vertical slit at each breast, possibly for adjusting the fit; small muff suspended from waist.
Engraving from *Civitates Orbis Terrarum*. Braun & Hogenburg.

STOMACHERS, FOREPARTS, FORESLEEVES. The wardrobes of our ancestors regularly included a number of detachable pieces inspired by a sound economic principle. It must be borne in mind that such portions of the apparel as were not intended to be displayed were as a rule made of coarse, strong material wholly devoid of ornament. The *stomacher* was an ornamental, shaped front destined to fill the front opening of the gown from breast to fork, conveying a false impression of an underlying corset. It lent itself to elaborate needlework and was apt to be the most highly decorated portion of the attire, being often supplied for greater pomp with a pair of detachable *foresleeves* to match. The stomacher assumed its most elaborate forms after 1600. It was very long and curved outward in a spatulate point as may be seen in numerous portraits of Dutch wives by Frans Hals, Thomas de Keyser, etc. The *forepart* was an apron-like piece of rich material for insertion in the front opening of the skirt. Mounted on to a petticoat of common stuff, it was an economical substitute for a whole garment of finer quality.

HEAD-DRESS. *French Hood.* This (with modifications) retains its popularity well into the 'eighties, becoming less fashionable as the 17th century advanced. The term comes now to be applied to a stiffened-out caul-like covering for the back of the head and prolonged forward to cover the ears from which depends a broad, folded tail, capable of being turned up and brought forward over the crown. This tail is a distinctive feature of the "French hood", as are the upper and lower borders, often jewelled (Fig. 32).

Cauls were a network of goldsmiths work, hair, or silk net, often worn over a silk lining. These cauls in Elizabeth's time were apt to be highly ornamental, being adorned with bands of gold lace, bows of ribbon, pearls, etc. This type of head-dress figures in numerous Elizabethan sepulchral effigies (best shown in *kneeling* figures) and brasses.[1]

32. English variety of French hood. *c.* 1545.
Princess Mary Tudor.
Hans Eworth (?)

The "Mary Stuart" hood was a linen or lawn head-dress, wired at the front into a curve which dipped over the forehead (Pl. 8). Its name derives from the portraits of Mary, Queen of Scots. In the case of widows especially, a gathered veil of fine lawn hung from the back of the head-dress. This type of head-dress nearly always covers the ears more or less, and, in its showier variants, has an edging and inlays of lace; though even ladies of rank were apt to rest content with plain coifs of finest lawn. Embroidery too was used to embellish it. Till the very close of the 16th century the "Mary Stuart" head-dress was relatively small and close-fitting; thenceforward the laced front, cut in deep "vandykes", was more upright and of wider spread. The crown, set backwards to enclose the coiled and braided "bun" of hair, was now often surrounded by an upright band of vandyked lace like a palisade.

Thin black silk and *cyprus* (similar to crape) were also used for such caps and veils, for widows and mourning generally.

The arched hood (Fig. 33) was worn, particularly out of doors and often

[1] To all who have not already put the idea in practice I cannot too warmly recommend a methodical, reasoned out study in detail of Elizabethan-Jacobean sepulchral effigies—again in particular the kneeling ones, where you can examine *the back* of the figure—in the choir of, say, Westminster Abbey. You can often learn more from one figure than from a dozen such books as the present.

when mourning or attending a funeral, from the 1580's : after 1620 it was more and more restricted to mourning wear by the elderly. It could be worn alone or over another head-dress.

Veils. A veil or headrail of fine gauze was pretty commonly appended to other forms of head-dress behind or worn thus independently. Sometimes it had a thin wire running through the top hem. This formed a high arch over the head, whence the headrail hung free over the shoulders. They were often edged by a narrow border of lace, pearls, etc. Alternatively

33. Large arched hood, decorated in centre. 1614.
Tomb figure.
Exeter Cathedral.

34. A countrywoman. Plain loose gown, no farthingale, tied by sash at waist; low arched neckline and pleated or gathered partlet; "Bowler"-hat over under-cap. 1587.
From a brass in Walton-on-Thames Church.

the wired arch might take the form of a single or multiple-lobed collar behind the head. Cf. latest portraits of Elizabeth and of Mary Stuart.

Imitation of male modes. All or nearly all the forms of head-dress already enumerated among masculine wear were worn in a more or less modified form by women also, more particularly for riding and travelling (Fig. 34). Usually they are somewhat reduced in size. Although examples are found worn in the highest ranks and often highly ornate, they are by no means a usual feature of formal apparel : from the 1560's no head covering at all, even out of doors, was considered quite correct.

Other varieties. There can be no pretence to exhaust the countless varieties of head-dress affected by the women of the Shakespearian age within our present limits. Apart from national modes, with all their social and regional variants, we should have to take account of features due to individual taste whose name is legion. The reader can only be advised to study the books and monographs recommended in the *Bibliography* and to amplify the information acquired by judicious study of the pictorial evidence indicated, bearing in mind the advice that accompanies that section.

HAIR. In the early years of the period the hair, parted in the centre, is waved or curled or puffed out from the temples. Note that throughout the changes that succeed one another in female coiffure two features remain pretty constant: the front hair is dressed *off* the forehead and temples and the back hair is braided in a thick plait and wound in a flat "bun" or chignon. The favourite fashion in the 'sixties and 'seventies was that known in France as the *raquette* or *ratepenade*. In this the hair above the brows, instead of being simply waved or curled, was strained back over a wire frame rising in a tall hoop on either side of the forehead and sinking to a rounded point in the centre. Sometimes the central portion of the wire, uncovered, was twisted into forms which, combined with the wide arches at the sides, distinctly suggests in outline a bat in flight. Hence doubtless the name *ratepenade* (or *ratepenache* a provincial French term for "bat"). But already from about 1570 a modified form was competing for favour: in this the front hair is not parted in the centre but forms a continuous roll from ear to ear, arched at the sides with a slight "dip" in the middle. This mode, in a steadily more pronounced form, retained its vogue right through the 'eighties and examples occur even in the 'nineties. It is of constant occurrence on our English sepulchral effigies.

Seen from in front, the *raquette* coiffure lends the face a heart-shaped contour. In France especially, the tendency from *c.* 1580 was for the hair to be dressed over pads rather than wires, and for the whole crown of the head to be curled and built up into a broad and lofty erection. It should be remembered that the use of false hair, variously dyed, was pretty general. In this country *c.* 1600–15, a tall hair style dressed over wire or a pad produced an elongated egg-head appearance. About 1595 the coiffure affected by Gabrielle d'Estrées, the short-lived favourite of Henri IV of France, had its fleeting moment of popularity. It is a very individual style, not easy to describe in words. Suffice it to remark that from in front it tends to remind one of one variety of the 15th century "heart shaped" head-dress. For the rest of the period the hair above the crown mostly forms an egg-shaped mass, which seems to foreshadow certain styles popular about 1770. From the 'eighties onward the ladies' hair is increasingly adorned with knots and bands of ribbon, lace and jewels.

FOOTGEAR. Except with the ankle-length skirts of *c.* 1605-20 these are rarely in evidence. In any case except for size there was little or no distinction between the two sexes. Thick-soled *pantoffles* were largely worn by women to increase their apparent stature. In the early 17th century,

35. Elevation and section of Venetian courtesan, showing chopines and drawers. Late 16th century.
Contemporary engraving. Musée de Cluny, Paris.

and perhaps in the later years of the 16th, cork soles and wedges on shoes had a like effect; although in both cases a practical use was to raise the feet in wet weather. Despite Hamlet's reference to *chopines*, I cannot find that this odd form of shoe, with its towering, pedestal-like sole, ever " caught on " except in Italy and to a less extent in Spain. In this country it was very rare and confined to the early 17th century. In fact, its extreme development seems to have been confined to Venice[1] (Fig. 35).

LINEN, CUTWORK, LACE. Neckwear and wrist-wear apart, *lingerie* at this date still plays a relatively subordinate part, although its rapidly improving quality was in the ensuing age to lend it first-rate importance.

[1] Travellers to that city always seem amazed at the stilt-like *cioppini*.

Lawn and cambric were coming into favour and "cutwork" was fast developing into lace of different kinds. It should be remembered that our forefathers had little mind to waste fine materials or ornaments where they could not be freely displayed and the fashions of this date (previous to *c.* 1610) did not yet lend themselves to an overlavish display of body-linen. Hence the enduring popularity of décolleté modes which permitted an increased show of fine linen embellished with embroidery and lace (borders and/or insertions).

36. Under propper, supportasse, or rebato for supporting large ruffs and standing bands: common to both sexes. *c.* 1630. Engraving by Wenzel Hollar.

All the forms of ruff, cuff and band found in male costume were equally adapted to female wear. In addition there were certain forms peculiar to the sex. Till the 'seventies the frill of the high chemise collar is frequently more or less widely open in front. As early as the 'fifties—though this is unusual till after 1570—with low-necked bodices a separate ruff edges the décolletage from side to side, rising fan-like behind the head, a fashion that increasingly disputed favour in courtly circles with the closed "cartwheel" ruff. The "cartwheel" was worn with both high and low necklines. From the 'eighties exposed bosoms become more and more common and about 1610 the V-shaped décolletage is sometimes so deep as to leave the breasts wholly bare. About the same period (i.e. 1580) appears a tall wired-out collar of similar fan-like contour but minus pleats. This collar was generally lace trimmed. The "fan" is sometimes fully extended, like a peacock's tail, but towards 1610 is also found, as it were, half-closed. Even beneath the "cartwheel" ruff the low-cut bodice often exposes the bosom.[1]

Details of supports for ruffs, starch, etc., are as for men's (Fig. 36).

Falling bands were not apparently an Englishwoman's fashion during this period.

Lace, lawn, etc., wrist-ruffs, or ruffles, similar to men's were worn with ruffs, and from 1580, turned-back cuffs could be worn with ruffs or collars.

UNDERCLOTHES and STOCKINGS. The *farthingale* has been noted already. In addition to the completely encircling cages and rolls there

[1] The "cartwheel" is, no doubt for this purpose, sometimes allowed to gape open in front in a Λ-shape over the breast.

was also a semicircled farthingale from about 1580 which was attached to the hinder regions only, in the manner of a large bustle. By the beginning of the 17th century the bum-roll and the semicircle were considered unfashionably plebeian.

The *chemise* or *smock* was the principal undergarment, worn next the body, and showed little apparent variation for many years. It is impossible to tell from paintings the exact design of this garment in the 16th century, but by the early 17th it followed the lines of a man's shirt, without the side vents.[1] Some chemises had a collar, which by mid 17th century had become high, worn loosely tied and exposed to view, or less high, with a frill which appears at the top of the bodice of the dress ; sometimes it is seen inside the ruff. Embroidery on the collar was like that of a man's shirt. With the décolletage of the low-necked bodice a low, wide-necked chemise was worn, with little appearing. Again embroidery decorated the neck line, and also frilling (Fig. 37). Sleeves, which were long and full, but often gathered at the wrists, were also embroidered in many cases. To the gathered wrist-bands would be attached the ruffles or cuffs.

37. Chemise with frill and embroidered braid at neck ; full sleeves gathered into wrist-bands. *c.* 1600.
Mary Magdalene. Caravaggio.

The smock was usually of linen ; cambric or holland. Silk was occasionally used. Heavily perfumed smocks attempted to avoid lack of comment by even one's best friends.

The *waistcoat*, of linen, velvet, woollen cloth, etc., was apparently, in the 16th century, like a man's, and was often extensively embroidered, in which case it was probably exposed to view, at least in the privacy of the home. Its relationship to the jacket is dubious.

Corsets have been previously mentioned, and were not in great evidence : their use with a boned bodice was supererogatory. One satirist of the time mentions them as

[1] See the specimen in the London Museum (A21968). The Metropolitan Museum of Art, New York, has an Italian example of the late 16th century, which has apparently been re-made or repaired at a later date.

"... privie coats by art made strong,
With bones and steels and such like ware."
Philip Gosson, 1591

but little is known of their construction or use at this period.

Knickers, or *drawers*, as before stated, were unknown in this country during the period under review. Italian women wore "silke or linnen breeches under their gownes", according to Fynes Morison in the early years of the 17th century. The only illustration I have come across (Fig. 35) shows a very substantial garment indeed; the wearers are stated to be Venetian ladies of the town.

The *petticoat* (this word in the 16th and 17th centuries also applied to the kirtle or skirt). In 1585 Englishwomen are said to have worn three cloth gowns or petticoats one over another. When worn underneath it is naturally an "under-petticoat", and in such a sense is the word used here. It appears that the petticoat was waist-length and fastened by points to the bodice, after the fashion of male hose. Petticoats were of cloth, serge, taffeta, silk, etc. Red was a popular colour. Presumably worn by the fashionable lady between the smock and the farthingale, in the case of the poorer classes it, and the farthingale, might be dispensed with altogether.

Stockings and garters. Stockings were at first tailored of cloth—silks for the rich, wool for the poor—but knitted stockings, again silk or wool, were rapidly replacing the cloth ones. Like other articles of clothing the 16th-century stocking was often elaborately decorated with embroidery. Colours were varied and clocks were sometimes present. The length of the stocking was to or just above the knee.

The stockings (or hose) were kept in place by garters of list, silk, etc., tied below the knee. Garters also were often embroidered and finished off with fringes or aglets at the ends, despite the universal concealment of the legs within the voluminous skirt.

ACCESSORIES. Women's *gloves* resemble men's. Rich laced or fringed *handkerchiefs* appear, in addition to more practical calico and holland ones. *Fans* are at first of feathers (sometimes enclosing a tiny mirror, the familiar folding type dating from the 'eighties) (Figs. 29 and 38). The feather fan is said not to have been favoured in Spain. Other materials were silk and straw: these fans were often, in fact, hand fire-screens. In Italy apparently originated a peculiar rigid variety with a long handle, in the shape of a small banner. *Hair-dye, paint* and *powder* grew in favour. *Jewellery* of all kinds (largely sham) was sprinkled over the whole person on state occasions. Close-fitting *masks* and half-masks were used when travelling, and walking abroad, both to hide one's identity and preserve the complexion. Often they were garnished inside with a very short cord ending in a button. When the teeth were closed on the cord, the button held the mask in place. Long *gold chains* were variously slung about the neck or formed a girdle with one end hanging low in front. *Girdles* were also often of ribbon or silk. They might support a cross, a locket, a fan or a small mirror. Sometimes a muff or fur stole was attached : the *stole* might be the skin of a martin or sable, lined with satin or velvet, the head and paws mounted in gold and precious stones. This could be worn as a boa, but the German name, *Flohpelzchen*, implies a more prosaic purpose.

38. French. Type of Mary Stuart hood: Spanish-type farthingale skirt; hooded cloak with wide sleeves; feather fan. 1570's.
Contemporary engraving, after *The Pictorial Encyclopedia of Fashion*, 1968.

Muffs were of fur or silk, and were fairly small (Figs. 26 and 31). *Purses* in the form of small bags with a drawstring, and *pomanders* were also attached to the girdle.

From the end of the 16th century *aprons* were worn at home, and very elegant ones even at Court in the early 17th century. Bibbed aprons were worn by working women.

Mufflers, squares of material folded diagonally and worn over the lower part of the face, served the same purposes as masks.

CHAPTER IV

1. FOREIGN CHARACTERISTICS
2. ARMOUR

1. FOREIGN CHARACTERISTICS

English fashions of the Elizabethan age were influenced by Continental modes, especially in the upper ranks of society, and various importations were made from Spain, France, Germany and the Netherlands, etc. Names such as Spanish farthingale, French farthingale, Dutch cloak, etc., show the extent of this influence. In considering English costume at this time, then, some attention must be paid to these foreign modes.

In addition, when approaching Shakespeare's plays it is to be remembered that various of these have a Continental setting, and might well be dressed partly at least, showing some of the distinctive national characteristics. It is hardly feasible in a book of this size to attempt any detailed analysis of the costume of the several nations; the more so that, in respect of the people at large, every little state or district on the Continent would have its distinctive *regional* features. On the other hand, except in remote country parts, among the better classes the fashions in civilized Europe were broadly the same, especially for men. In fact, very often it is not possible to determine the nationality of contemporary portraits from the mere costume, which might belong indifferently to England, France, the Netherlands, Spain or Italy.

39. French. Slashed doublet and paned trunkhose: prominent cod-piece. 1570's.
After *A History of Costume*, Carl Köhler.

There are, however, certain distinctive features which may be pointed out as guideposts to nationality. In the Netherlands the costume of the well-to-do is directly moulded at first upon Spain; from 1580 to 1600 there is a strong French tone ; while after 1600 the two influences coalesce (especially among the women) and a definite national type is perceptible.

France borrowed her fashions almost as widely as England, but contrived so to edit them as to give them a character of their own, especially *c.* 1575–95. (Fig. 39). Peasecods, tight lacing and bombast are carried to extremes. A certain calculated negligence was fashionable in the 'eighties :

40. Venetian. Jerkin with slashes on breast worn over pinked doublet; thigh-length cloak; breeches with three buttons at the knee; tall-crowned bonnet. *c.* 1580.
After *A History of Costume*, Carl Köhler.

41. Venetian. Gown as worn by the nobility, scholars, official classes, etc. Sleeves very full at elbows. Mid 16th century.
After *A History of Costume*, Carl Köhler.

the garments are left in part unfastened, one sleeve in use the other hanging free, the stockings half unrolled, etc. Women largely copy the Italian décolletage. Long *reiter* cloaks and broad leaved hats are in much favour. In Spain, black is your general wear, the long-waisted doublet close-fitting with long tight sleeves. Except the clergy, all wear ruffs increasing in size, and mostly wide trunkhose, tall bag-shaped caps and shoes slashed crosswise (Fig. 12). The short cape with a hood is typical of Castille.

Elderly ladies' heads were commonly shrouded in nun-like linen veils. The bodices are high-necked and ornamental points freely lavished over the person.

In considering Italy it should be remembered how powerful the Spanish influence was there: half the courts modelled themselves on Madrid. On the whole, so far as they were free from Spain's example, the Italians favoured easier, less exaggerated styles, simpler in cut and more sparing of trimmings (Figs. 40 and 41). The men largely favoured falling bands and venetians; the women bare heads and low necks, nor were verdingales in evidence. Venice in particular refused to subscribe to Spanish modes; the open gowns and little caps of the men, the horned *coiffure*, open bodice and *chopines* of the women are in a class by themselves (Fig. 35).

42. German. A merchant dressed for travel: slop-hose and stockings cross-gartered: Spanish cloak with hood; cap or bonnet, possibly of fur. 1576.

Contemporary engraving: after *The Pictorial Encyclopedia of Fashion.*

Typically German modes were loose and untidy, often the men's garments were slittered almost to rags by indiscriminate, wholesale slashing (Fig. 8). Pickadils were scattered over the costume to excess. Green and yellow were much in favour. These features tend to diminish and vanish with the end of the 16th century. The merchant class favoured a more business-like garb (Fig. 42). The costume of the Swiss at large was close kin to the German, but is notable for being generally a full generation behind other nations.[1] The true German doublet was rather short in the body and the girdlestead ran straight round the waist without the pointed dip in front: a mode which enjoyed a certain brief vogue in western Europe *c.* 1595–1605. In Central Europe bombast and busks were regarded as foreign and papistical fashions, though Lutheran preachers were as severe on the native as on foreign modes. Furs too were more popular in Germany than in the west or south. Characteristic features, of their women's dress are little, flat, mannish caps, furred shoulder-tippets and narrow pleated aprons.

[1] E.g. the full-length portraits at Basel of a man and his wife. Although dated 1564, they wear the fashions of the time of Maximilian I (died 1519).

II. ARMOUR

Shakespeare's work was produced in an age during which defensive armour was rapidly declining alike in quality and quantity. During the 16th and 17th centuries the infantry comprised both pikemen and musketeers (also referred to as the "shot") (Fig. 43). In order to afford adequate protection from the increasing efficiency of firearms armour now had to be made so cumbrous as to be intolerable. On the other hand the "shot" were still for the most part imperfectly developed in their operations, and armour, if not impenetrable, could yet offer a very useful degree of protection.

43. Spanish soldiers. Two Officers, musketeer, and pikeman. Note absence of armour (one officer only wears a morion). Late 16th- or early 17th-century.
Palace of Viso del Marques, Spain.

It was therefore a hotly debated point to what extent it should be retained. Nowhere more than in England was there a growing disposition to scrap one part after another.

Cap-à-pie armour was mainly reserved to the tilt yard, or for pageantry or (particularly) for inclusion in one's portrait. It is often sumptuously decorated with engraving, gilding, embossing and damascening as if to camouflage its growing senility. Nevertheless it provided acceptable evidence of a gentleman's wealth and military rank. Such was the splendid

PLATE 5

Jerkin with sleeves closed by ribbon ties, decorated with slashes ; full trunkhose ; decorated girdle and hangers ; standing band or golilla with band strings left exposed ; cuffs ; embroidered night-cap. 1613.

Sir Phineas Pett : Jan de Critz.
National Portrait Gallery, London.

embossed cap-à-pie armour of Alexander Farnese by the great armourer Lucio Piccinino now at Vienna. Yet by his own account,[1] whether on land or sea, Farnese was content to fight armed merely in a stout cuirass, a morion and a strong target. It should however be noted that even field-armour was often much decorated, so that it is no easy matter at times to draw a sharply defined distinction between armour for the field and for mere display.

Tilt-armour need hardly detain us now ; so we will confine ourselves to armour and weapons for "the field" (=war). Considering the varied aspects of warfare presented in his plays, Shakespeare's technical vocabulary of its material adjuncts is singularly meagre. Despite his vaunted universality, his acquaintance with its practical details was evidently sketchy : it would not be possible from his works to reconstruct the figure of the contemporary warrior.

Before Shakespeare's career was ended the "man at arms" had given place to the "lancier" and "cuirassier" who henceforward constituted the "heavy" cavalry, while the warrior encased in steel from head to heel was becoming an isolated figure.

Cap-à-pie armour was however still such a *living memory* that we may fairly assume it to have been a freely accepted property of the Shakespearian stage. How far the warrior of the plays was expected to conform on the boards with the real thing must needs remain an open question : a good deal may well have been taken for granted, unless postulated by the "business" of the scene. It should not be forgotten that full armour was not only cumbersome, but slow to adjust and discard. Moreover it necessitated special underwear.

It is rather odd and regrettable, if only for variety's sake, that stage and screen should not more freely avail themselves of opportunities of showing military underwear, such as was the usual garb when soldiers expected to be summoned to action. It could be used to good effect. For wear beneath the cuirass there was the *arming-doublet* of stout buff-leather. It was mostly rather short, padded and quilted—especially upon the shoulders and below the waist to mitigate the pressure of the armour. To it were tied by points either *gussets* of mail protecting the chinks in the armour at shoulder and armpit, or complete

[1] Verbally to Jakob Hannibal von Hohenems in 1578–79. *Target* usually = the round shield known in France as a *rondache*. Hohenems' actual words are "*aine starke prust, ain morian und ain rundel*".

mail-sleeves to the wrist which lined the gaps in the *vambraces* or replaced this part of the armour. Generally an *apron* of mail guarded the undefended crutch of the wearer : this was securely tied to the arming-doublet.

The head below the helmet was commonly protected by a close-fitting, quilted *arming-cap* for wear under the helmet (which already had a quilted lining), having side-lappets to tie beneath the chin.

Shoes (lacing up the inside) covered with mail and having solid plate toe-caps often replaced the jointed *sabatons*.

Where greaves and sabatons were still worn, they were often donned over boots of pliable leather, reinforced with strips of mail at all the vulnerable points.

By Shakespeare's time the armour of the legs and feet had been generally replaced by high riding-boots. For the rest we will content ourselves here with general remarks : merely remarking that the military writers and mustermasters of the period are at some variance in their views of the proper equipment for the different classes of troops. Only over the men-at-arms and the " armed pikes " are they pretty well agreed. In practice there seems in England to have been little uniformity, as may be seen from Sir John Smythe's criticism of the host assembled at Tilbury in 1588.

Armour of this date is :

1. " White " or " milled " i.e. of blank, polished steel.

2. Black and white : groundwork black with reserved bands of bright steel, sunken or in relief.

3. Russeted.

4. " Sanguine " or " purple " = blued : The term arises from the purplish-red reflections on the deep blue surface.

HEADPIECES. The correct wear for men-at-arms is the visored head-piece completely encasing the head and known at the period as a *close helmet* or *field headpiece*, to which were riveted extra *lames* or " splints " to protect the neck (Fig. 44a). The movable front was composed of three pieces : " the viser and the two baviers " (*visors* and *beavers*), which could be raised severally or together and worked freely on the same pair of pivots. They are often referred to jointly as the *beaver* or *beavers*. Strictly speaking the field headpiece comprises : (1) the *skull* or *basnet* encasing the cranium, with gorget-plates attached ; (2) the *visor*, with transverse slits (*sights*) for vision ; (3) the *ventaille* (or upper-beaver) perforated for breathing ; (4) the *buffe* (or nether-beaver) with attached gorget-plates, covering chin and throat : all these plates fitted into one another.

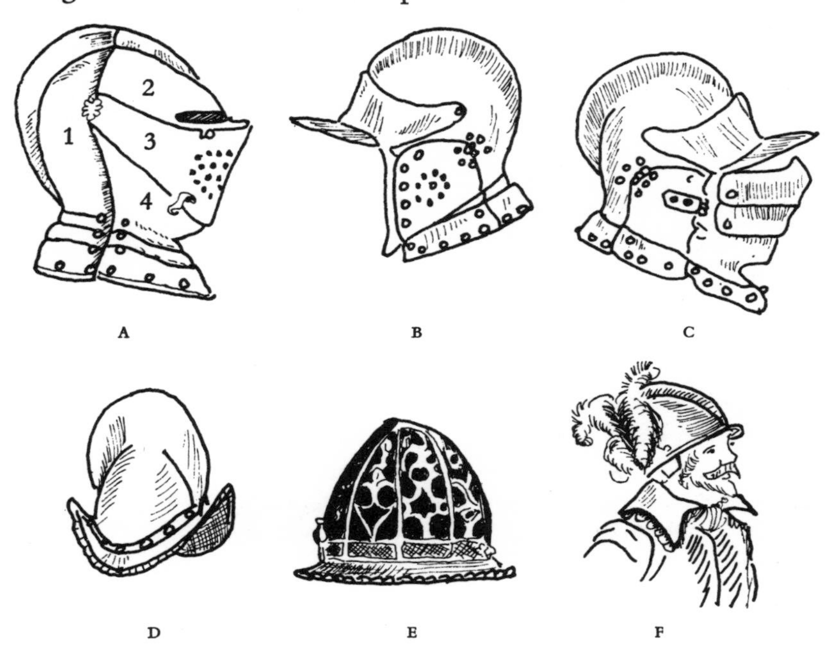

44. Helmets. (A) Italian close helmet *c.* 1585. The numbered parts are : (1) skull or basnet, (2) visor, (3) upper beaver, (4) nether beaver. (B) Burgonet. (C) Burgonet with collapsible beaver. (D), (E), (F) Italian and Spanish morions.

After the sketch in the original edition.

(There is a problem in connection with the armour of Hamlet's ghost, which seems to have escaped the critics. Clearly he wears a *close helmet* :

> " Ham : Then saw you not his face ?
> Hor : Oh yes, my Lord, *he wore his beaver up*.
> Ham : His beard was grizzled, no ?
> Hor : It was, as I have seen it in his life,
> A sable silvered."

But the portion of the helmet *covering the cheeks and chin,* although movable, is quite incapable of being " worn up " in any form of headpiece that I know. Only the *ventaille* or upper beaver could be so *worn* (carrying with it the *visor*), whereby the front of the face, from eyebrow to mouth, would alone be revealed. Of the hair of the face the *moustache alone* is visible. We must suppose then either that " beard " here = moustache, or that Horatio deduces from the colour of the latter that of the hair on the cheeks, *which he could not see*. The only illustrations of the play that I recall which illustrate the point are those by Kenny Meadows.)

By *burgonet* is meant " a certaine kind of head peece, either for foote or horſemen, covering the head and *part of* the face and cheeke " (Barret, 1598). It protected the nape, had hinged cheekplates and a projecting brim (*fall*) like an eyeshade in front (Fig. 44b). This was the accepted headpiece of the light cavalry and pikemen, and—doubtless on account of its " classical " outline and practical virtues—a general favourite with officers of every arm. Moreover, by the addition at will of an independent beaver or *buffe*, it could be converted into a protection well-nigh as complete as the *close helmet* (Fig. 44c).

The *morion* was the infantry headpiece *par excellence*. It is remarkable that Shakespeare nowhere mentions it, seeing that of all helmets of his day it was likely to be most familiar to him. In the closing years of the 16th century it even ousted the *burgonet* as the chosen headpiece of the " armed pikes ". Although it would seem to have varied a good deal in outline, the only forms which we can define with any confidence are the *comb-morion* (Fig. 44d) and the *Spanish morion* (Fig. 44e). The latter is the helmet which antiquaries have rather arbitrarily identified with the " cabasset ".[1]

Do not, whatever you do, wear your morion tilted *forward*, as so often happens on stage and film alike. It should be worn either upright or with a backward tilt.

In both forms the brim may sweep up to a sharp point fore and aft like the " horns " of a crescent moon, or may be narrow and flat. It was sometimes secured under the chin by broad, plated cheekbands, sometimes by strap and buckle, or a *scarf* (tie of textile material, knotted like a cravat)—usually red. Plumes may be worn (Fig. 44f).

I have not so far been able to come to any conclusion as to the nature of the helmet known at this date as a *sallet*. The true sallet went out early in the 16th century.

[1] " Spanish " burgonets, like " Spanish " morions, are distinguished by their pointed crowns.

> The suggestion that Shakespeare's use of the word is a mere piece of deliberate archaism is negatived by other contemporary texts.

As for the term *cask* (or *casque*) one can only say that it applies to an open helmet, presumably similar to the burgonet; though "the very casques that did affright the air at Agincourt" evidently refers to head-pieces in general.

CORSLET (Half-armour). So identified were pikemen with the corslet that "corslet", "corsleteer", "pike" and "pikeman" were virtually interchangeable terms. The 16th-century corslet when "complete" (or "furnished") comprised "good curates (cuirass = back and breast) for their bodies, tasses for their thighs, poldrones and vambraces for their shoulders and arms, burgonites for their heads" (Styward 1581).

> (It is doubtless by an oversight that Styward has omitted to specify "collars or gorgets for their necks" for this was an indispensable item; serving in fact to support the whole body-armour, *pauldrons* and sometimes *vambraces*.)

In addition the hide-bound precisians would prescribe gauntlets; though these had ceased to be obligatory since Philip and Mary. The troops thus fully armed were known as "armed pikes" or "ordinary pikes" and mostly fought in the first four ranks "where sometimes Captains, Lieutenants, Sergeants and Cavalliers of bandes be placed with Pikes and is the place for Gentlemen to serve in . . ." (Garrard 1591). "Cavalliers of bandes" were otherwise known as "gentlemen of a company". The remainder of the pikemen were termed "extraordinary pikes" or "dry pikes", and were more sparingly accoutred: either in "the forepart of a Corslet and a Headpeece . . . or a good light Jack or a plate Coate" (Garrard). These "jacks" were "quilted and covered over with leather, fustian or canvas, over thicke plates of iron that are sowed in the same . . ." (Harrison, 1577). Among the pikemen were posted a few ranks of halberdiers or billmen, armed in corslets or in brigandines. The *brigandine* (rapidly going out of fashion) was a flexible jacket covered with leather, canvas or even velvet, lined with overlapping riveted plates, the heads of the rivets forming a pattern of studs on the outer surface. It was of finer make and material than the jack. The halberdier wearing a corslet, might wear mail sleeves in place of vambraces. Ensigns of infantry might dispense at will with *tasses*. Sergeants carried a halberd and wore no tasses. Arquebusiers wore morions with brigandines, jacks or occasionally shirts (or only sleeves) of mail ; sometimes the morion alone. By Shakespeare's time the musketeer had entirely discarded defensive armour, even the headpiece being replaced by " a fair hat and plume ". A captain of infantry, when marching through towns at the head of his company, should be armed with a *corslet complete* and carry his pike or partisan on his shoulder ; his burgonet being *worn* by his page who bears his *target* (round shield) before or beside him. In hand-to-hand fighting he would use target and sword.

> For stage or film purposes the captain accompanied by his page wearing his helmet and bearing his target would be a novel and striking figure. Mounted officers too had pages riding by them in their helmets and carrying their gauntlets and lance.

Plate 3 shows Philip II of Spain in such a corslet richly etched or engraved.

The Spanish infantry included a certain number of *targeteers* who fought with short swords. Several English military writers strongly advocate the employment of such troops, as being superior to billmen and halberdiers.

Towards 1610 the pikemen had for the most part discarded pauldrons and vambraces.

Although the term " corslet " was primarily associated with the heavily armed infantry—both Barret and Florio describe it identically : " the armour for a foote-souldier complete "—it is also applicable to the fighting kit of the light horsemen, which comprises practically the self-same pieces. The " arquebusier on horseback " (mounted infantry, presently known as *dragoons*) had normally no armour but a *morion*. The arming of the *stradiots* varied too much in different countries for description here ; but *pistoliers* and *carbines* wore neither *tasses* nor *vambraces* and one gauntlet only for the bridle hand. In lieu of *vambraces* they might have mail-sleeves.

MONNIONS, ELBOW-GAUNTLETS and ALMAIN COLLARS. All the military writers of the period confirm Barret's definition of the term *vambrace* : " the arming [of plate] *from the pouldron downward to the hand-wrest* " (=the wrist) ; that is, it includes the plates covering both fore-arm and upper-arm, united by the metal elbow-guard which the writers of the time take for granted, but for which Mr Ffoulkes has coined the useful term " elbow-cop " on the analogy of the *knee-cop* specified in 16th-century texts. Many for convenience supplied the absence of vambraces by pauldrons and gauntlets of a particular fashion. Reference to the *moignons* of French and *mugnoni* of Italian contemporary writers sufficiently explains the very rare term *monnions* in certain English texts. It is clear that it refers to a defence of overlapping plates covering only the point of the shoulder and outside of the upper-arm. It frequently reached to the elbow. The *elbow-gauntlet* had a narrow cuff prolonged to protect the point of the elbow and overlap the *monnion* ; the combination made up in a measure for the lack of vambraces. Where the gorget had the *monnions* riveted to it, it was known as an Almain *collar*. The armour of Sir John Smythe in the Tower still has its " Almain collar ", as described in the inventory of 1611, and Saulx-Tavannes' *Memoirs* refer to " *un grand haussecol* À L'ALLEMANDE *portant ses moignons* ".

Note that the collar or gorget, especially when handsomely decorated, was not infrequently worn in semi-mufti.

Armour terminology. In a book of this type, not addressed to the specialist, it might seem pedantic to insist on the importance of a correct nomenclature.

Here it may be as well once for all to enumerate the component parts of a complete " field-harness " at this date.

1. The *collar* or *gorget* for the neck.
2. The *cuirass* (composed of *breast* and *back*)—for the trunk.
3. The *tasses* (a pair) appended to the breastplate, to defend the thigh.
4. The *pauldron* for the shoulder.
5. The *vambrace* for the whole arm.
6. The *gauntlet* for the hand.
7. The *cuish* (*cuisse* or *cuisset*) or defence for thigh and knee (unconnected with cuirass).
8. The *greave* for the leg below the knee.
9. The *sabaton* for the foot.
10. The *headpiece* explains itself. The word *helmet* then denoted a " close " headpiece (i.e. with visor and beaver).

Even among specialists a number of " technical " terms are current for which it is impossible to make out a case. " Why ", the reader will object, " cavil over mere words ? Provided they convey a definite meaning, do they not serve every practical purpose ? " Granted, so long as you are content to study only modern writers on armour. Let us suppose, however, that the keen enquirer is desirous of consulting contemporary authorities. It is safe to say that he will realize with a shock how little the armour-jargon picked up (often at second-hand) from Meyrick, Planché,

Boutell and their progeny (even to this day) will help him to understand writers of the 16th and 17th centuries. He will look in vain for the familiar " soleret ", " espalière ", " cabasset ", " tasset ", " jamb ", etc., and find instead genuine old English words like *sabaton*, *pauldron* or (possibly) *monnion*, *Spanish morion*, *tasse*, and *greave*.

(Note that the distinction suggested by many modern writers between *taces* and *tassets* is purely fictitious. *Taces*, *taches*, *taisses* or *tasses*—" tassets " is a later, Frenchified form—are synonymous words, denoting the flaplike guards that hung from the " skirt " of the breastplate over the thighs. They were buckled, more rarely riveted, or (later) hinged to the *skirt* (to which the aforesaid writers would restrict the form *taces*). As for " tuiles " and " tuilettes ", armour till Meyrick never knew of such a term. One had hoped it by now once and for all decently interred, thanks mainly to Mr C. R. Beard. Some confusion seems to exist—even in contemporary minds—between *tasse* and *cuish*. The solution is simple. Whether short or long enough to include *knee-caps*, the former is always a dependant (literally) of the breastplate, while the *cuish* is unconnected with it. By the beginning of the 17th century the tasses were often long enough to cover the knees, and replaced the cuishes entirely. Old English knows nothing of " soleret" : the regular term is *sabaton* which has *no* special reference to the splay-toed early Tudor variety. Except perhaps in the later poetry, the word *mail* in the old texts applied exclusively to the so-called " chain-armour ", and the manifold defences included under the heading " mail " by Meyrick and his followers are but so many figments of the Meyrickian brain. As for " chain mail " and—worse still—" plate mail ", as well talk of " round circles " and " cubic spheres" .)

ARMS and ARMOUR in use. In nothing perhaps are the limitations of cinematography more manifest than in attempts to present hand-to-hand fighting on a wholesale scale as practised in a vanished age. It is not within the scope of such a book as this to offer constructive criticism on the point. On the other hand the effect produced is obviously enormously enhanced if armies on the march or in battle are seen to manœuvre according to a definite plan. To this we shall return in the chapter on the " conduct " of costume.

STAVES. The word " staff " in contemporary references to weapons is apt to disconcert the uninitiated. It may fairly be applied to all offensive weapons composed of a metal head (axe, cutting blade, spike or what not) mounted on a long wooden shaft. With the exception of the *lance*, all such weapons (nowadays classed as " hafted weapons ") belong to pedestrians. Distinguished essentially by the shape of the iron heads, their variety is great. Merely bearing in mind that practically all are the ultimate evolution of the peace-time implements of the populace, we will here be content to mention :

The *halbert* is a combination of large axe-blade or chopper balanced by a projecting spike and topped by an elongated pike-head. It is the distinctive weapon of the sergeant and (in many cases) the ensign.

The *partisan* is reserved to officers (ensigns often excepted). Its head is shaped like a large trowel with two small pointed flukes projecting from the base.

The *three-grained staff* comprises weapons of the trident class, such as the *rawcon* which consists of a long rapier-like blade flanked by a pair of " addorsed " scythe-blades.

The *bill* whose head is a development of the common hedger and ditcher's tool.

The *voulge* (or *gleve* ?) which has a head like a great knife or cleaver tapering to a sharp point. German and Italian officers commonly carry it instead of the Western partisan.

Of all the infantry, however, the pikemen were held to be the élite. The pike was distinguished by its simplicity and its great length—16 to 18 feet. The head was of simple lancet form or else shaped like a four-square awl, and the metal was prolonged in a couple of long strips down the wooden shaft to prevent the head being cut off. On the stage pikes are usually far too short, just as other hafted weapons are too long.

BIBLIOGRAPHY TO CHAPTERS II, III AND IV

The following *modern* works may profitably be studied in connection with the matter of the foregoing chapters :

BARTON, Lucy : *Historic Costume for the Stage*. London, A. & C. Black, Ltd. 1937. Chaps. IX and XX contain useful practical suggestions for dressing this period. Also useful for earlier and later periods.

BŒHN, Max von : *Modes & Manners*. Vol. II: *The Sixteenth Century* (translated by Joan Joshua). London, Harrap 1932. Interesting pictorially.

KELLY, F. M. : *Shakespearian Dress Notes* in *Burlington Magazine*, 1916-1917.

KELLY, F. M. and R. SCHWABE : *Historic Costume, 1490-1790*, 2nd ed. London, Batsford 1929.

KELLY, F. M. and R. SCHWABE : *Short History of Costume and Armour*, 2 vols. Batsford 1931 (Vol. II). The portions relating to the "Spanish" modes contain valuable illustrations of Shakespeare's age.[1]

LINTHICUM, M. Channing : *Costume in the Drama of Shakespeare and his Contemporaries*. Oxford University Press 1936. The *real* importance of this book lies almost entirely in its wealth of references to contemporary documents. The illustrations are inadequate and misleading : for the most part not even contemporary.

MASON, Rupert : *Robes of Thespis*. London, Benn 1928. A sumptuously produced and illustrated book on costume-designing for the stage. A good deal of information on the treatment of Shakespeare in the past will be found in the section : *Historic or "Period" Costume*.

MORSE, H. K. : *Elizabethan Pageantry*. (The Studio Special Spring Number 1934.) A handy "Pictorial Survey . . . 1560-1620", well arranged, with a good glossary and bibliography

NORRIS, Herbert : *Costume and Fashion*. Vol. III : *The XVIth Century*. Dent 1938. A valuable stand-by ; the author has a practical working knowledge of his job.

The foregoing are English works, but some of the most valuable contributions to the subject have been foreign and to those capable of coping with them one can confidently recommend :

CHRISTENSEN, Sigrid Flamand : *Die männliche Kleidung in der süddeutschen Renaissance*. Berlin 1934.

DE JONGE, C. H. : *Bijdrage tot de Kennis van de Kleederdracht en de Nederlanden en de XVIc. eeuw* (in *Oud Holland* XXXVI-XXXVII, Amsterdam 1918-1919).

Deal solely with male attire, but are excellent within their limitations.

DER KINDEREN-BESIER, J. H. : *Mode-Metamorphosen. De Kleedig onzer Vooronders en de XVIc. eeuw*. Amsterdam 1933. One of the best essays yet published on its subject.

Although these last two books deal with the Netherlands, much of their matter is ground common to France and England.

THIENEN, Frithjof van : *Das Kostüm der Blütezeit Hollands*. (Vol. VI of *Kunstwissenschaftliche Studien*.) Berlin 1930. Dutch costume 1600-1620 is skilfully analysed on pp. 8-58. Offers much valuable information applicable to England and France.

[1] As much may be claimed for Vol. I of the last-named work with regard to earlier periods.

As regards arms, armour and military equipment in general, there seems to be no book on the market which gives a really comprehensive idea, with adequate illustration of its evolution from a purely military point of view and of the appearance at successive dates of the fighting man of all arms and ranks in the 16th and 17th centuries. Hewitt's *Ancient Armour and Weapons*, Oxford 1859-61, despite its indifferent illustrations, remains even now perhaps the best general treatise on the subject. There are a number of valuable monographs on isolated sections. The writings of the late Charles Buttin are especially full of useful information. Ffoulkes' *The Armourer and his Craft*, 1912, and *Survey of the Tower Armouries* are full of good stuff. Laking's *Record of European Armour*, 1920-1922, seems too exclusively directed to the rich private collector of *de luxe* examples to serve our purpose here. The published works of the late Lord Dillon, of Messrs Cripps-Day, Charles Beard and Sir J. Mann are likelier to be of help. The English version by the latter of Ct. Trapp's *catalogue raisonné* of the Churburg armoury is a model of its kind. As regards the *nomenclature* of arms and armour, the student is referred to Mr Beard's article "Armour and the *New English Dictionary*" in the *Connoisseur*, August 1928, p. 235, and Sir J. Mann's letter that followed *Ibid.*, October 1928, p. 121.

ICONOGRAPHY

For the age of Shakespeare in civilized Europe the works of the following artists are full of invaluable costume and armour details:

PAINTERS: (Italian) Bronzino, Moroni, Pulzone, Tintoretto, Zuccaro. (Netherlandish) Hans Eworth, Gerlach Flicke, Marcus Gheeraedts (senr. and junr.), Joris (George) Hoefnagel, Cornelis Ketel, Adriaen and Thomas Key, Nic. Lucidel, Lucas de Heere, Anthonis Mor (Sir Antonio More or Moro), Pourbus family, Lucas van Valckenburg, senr., John de Critz, Isaac Oliver, Paul van Somer. (Spanish) Alonso Sanchez Coello, Rolam de Mois, Christoval de Moraes, Juan Pantoja de la Cruz, Bartholome Gonzales, Felipe de Liaño, Pablo Vidal. (French) The Clouet school and allied painters: Le Mannier, J. de Court, A. Caron, Dumoustier, F. Quesnel. (German) Lutger and Hermann tom Ring, Jakob Seisenegger, Lucas Cranach, junr., Georg Pencz. (English) Nicholas Hilliard.

ENGRAVERS. De Bry family, Jost Amman,[1] Hendrick Goltzius, Tobias Stimmer, Wierix family, Crispin de Passe, J. de Gheyn, Frans Hogenberg, Tortorel and Perissim. A number of books of the 16th and early 17th centuries contain illustrations—woodcuts or copper plates—often of real documentary value. Sometimes it is a mere frontispiece or pictorial title-page, sometimes they are scattered

[1] Both Amman and Stimmer—once you get into the way of making allowance for the typically German element—are full of invaluable material.

through the book. Michael Eytzinger's (Aitzingerus) *Novus de Leone Belgico . . . Liber*, Cologne 1587, is one such. Another is Jan van der Noot's *Abrégé des douze livres Olympiaden*, Antwerp 1579. Turberville's two treatises on hunting and hawking, both published 1575, are further examples. We can but touch briefly on such volumes here, but the list could be indefinitely extended and the reader may care to follow up the hint further.

The second half of the 16th and first quarter of the 17th centuries was the age of the *album amicorum* of the travelling student, usually filled in part with water-colour drawings of the types seen in his wanderings; but also of a whole series of albums of engravings published in Italy, the Netherlands and Germany, depicting the costumes of the principal nations and cities of the known world. These vary much in documentary value, but none are worthless and some are thoroughly reliable records. We mention here as outstanding examples:

BERTELLI, Ferdinando: *Omnium fere gentium nostrae aetatis habitus*. Venice 1569.
BERTELLI, Pietro: *Diversarum nationum ornatus*. Padua 1594.
BOISSARD, J. J.: *Habitus variorum orbis gentium*. Malines 1581.
DE BRUYN, Abraham: *Omnium pene gentium imagines*. Cologne 1577; Second edition, Antwerp 1581.
VECELLIO, Cesare: *Degli habiti antichi et moderni*. Venice 1590.
WEIGEL Hans and Jost AMMAN: *Habitus praecipuorum populorum*. Nürnberg 1577.

On these contemporary costume-albums see Max von Bœhn: *Modes and Manners—II: The Sixteenth Century*, pp. 105-109.[1] Of Vecellio's book there is a French edition of 1857 by Lacombe, who has added to the Italian notices a translation of his own, while the original woodcuts have been redrawn—*not* to their advantage. His translation is thoroughly incompetent and this edition is not to be recommended.

(See also General Bibliography.)

[1] English edition (transl. Joan Joshua); Harrap 1932.

CHAPTER V

ON THE "NICE CONDUCT" OF PERIOD COSTUME

It seems generally to be assumed that, so long as the designer of the costumes for a period-production " knows his job ", and has at his disposal a competent costumier and property-maker, all the demands of the " show " are fully provided for so far as the wardrobe department is concerned. It is curious by the way to note how, if the particular production, in addition to being a box-office draw, awakes general admiration as a spectacle, the credit seems as a rule to be given unreservedly to the impresario ; whereas any shortcomings from the point of view of pictorial appeal are as likely as not visited upon the designer. On the other hand if, in spite of a thoroughly effective *mise-en-scène*, the particular piece fails as a commercial proposition, the excuse is likely to be made that " costume plays never pay ".

It would in point of fact be no great matter to show that this is a complete fallacy. Given a story sufficiently appealing in itself, handled by a thoroughly competent craftsman, and interpreted by a first-rate cast, the question of period will hardly arise. The play and the players will carry it triumphantly through *in the teeth of an inferior setting,* so long as the appeal of the play itself to the public is sufficiently strong.

That in the past money lavished upon a sumptuous period-production was apt to be wasted is only too true. The manager anxious to make a big splash wanted " names " which he imagined would pass upon the playbill as evidence that the whole affair had been " done regardless of expense ". Hence he entrusted the designing of the dress and properties to some fashionable artist whose knowledge of costume was often sketchy and his understanding of stage-requirements of the vaguest. The designer in such case, having had his designs passed for execution, was frequently content to leave their execution largely to the mercies of the costumier, whom he was too often incompetent to help or check efficiently. In such circumstances it is surprising how many times they contrived " to get away with it " to everyone's satisfaction.

Today, on the stage, screen and in television the situation has immeasurably improved. The designer thoroughly understands the costume of his period from a practical point of view. He knows the effects he intends to produce and the resources at his command. The costumier, too, not only knows his trade, but is most anxious to do justice to the designer's aims. Both are much better educated, historically than they used to be. In a word their collaboration is altogether satisfactory. So far all is well, and the ordinary layman might be disposed to imagine that success in this department is practically assured. Alas ! no ; we have left out of our account a most important factor : the actor. Only the intelligent designer can fully realize how powerfully the wearer of his costumes can contribute to their successful realization in action.

The Britons and Americans never seem quite at their ease in unfamiliar trappings. They seem to have an ingrained mistrust of the picturesque. The Englishman's normal ideal would seem to be to merge unnoticed into his background.[1] If his vocation entails the wearing of a more or less picturesque uniform, he is seldom happy till he has an opportunity to discard it in favour of a drab mufti. Your Guards' officer would not think of attending his own wedding otherwise than in a morning-coat, striped trousers and top hat. Contrast this with the custom of France where every guest, especially a kinsman, if entitled to wear military or naval uniform, is expected to appear in full parade-kit, not omitting a single decoration.

Nothing more naturally conduces to elegant attitudes and gestures than the free use of flowing draperies. Probably the picturesque garb of the Scottish Highlands sustained a greater loss than we realize when it renounced the use of the great belted plaid. Anyone who has seen a Dominican friar or a Benedictine monk in the pulpit will hardly fail to realize the dramatic value of the huge, flowing sleeves as against the more usual surplice and cassock. It is impossible with such a mass of drapery on the arms to make an abrupt, jerky movement.

An experienced actor of the old school once remarked that the chief handicap to the effective use of *costume* on the stage was the mere word in itself. This struck me as a profound truth. In England at least " costume " commonly suggests " fancy dress " or at the least " dressing up ". Even the man (this is less true of women) who makes no bones about donning unfamiliar raiment in his more expansive moments has a rooted sense

[1] This applies even to the extravagant and exotic garments worn now (1973) by some young—and not so young—people, which have become a sort of uniform for certain groups. The individual must respect the conventions of his fellows by wearing their conventional attire.

that he is after all merely playing the fool, much as when he puts on the paper cap out of a cracker at Xmas. As long as " costume " with us retains this sort of association we shall never succeed in carrying it off with any semblance of conviction. This knack of " carrying the thing off " is more often native to Frenchmen and Italians than to our own countrymen. I have often seen costumes only worthy of a " penny gaff " so triumphantly worn by a Latin that the ultimate impression was entirely satisfactory ; a faculty comparatively rare among Britons. If our stage-folk would banish the term " costume " from their vocabulary, and be content to speak of any and every dress worn for stage-purposes simply as " clothes " or " gear ", the actor would insensibly be led to think correctly of his costume, whatever the date and country, merely as his *normal working-dress.*

If the actor could from the outset rehearse his part in the actual costume in which he will eventually play it, I am convinced that the production would be materially benefited. The whole preparation and building up of his rôle, even without scenery, would become inseparable from the costume belonging to it. This, however, is in the nature of a counsel of perfection and, as things are, can never be more than a pious aspiration. Indeed the actor who receives his dress completed and ready for wear by the dress rehearsal is usually content. I have sometimes wondered, however, whether it might not be feasible to supply the company in a period-play with cheap substitute costumes from the first rehearsal onward : mere rough suggestions of the type of thing they are ultimately to wear. The real value of such a costume would be to accustom the actor from the outset to discard his ordinary street wear the moment he approached his stage-work. In many Schools of Drama the curriculum usually includes a course of instruction in the wearing of, and deportment in, period costume and there should be special attention paid to the correct use of accessories. In these matters it should be borne in mind that every age and nation has its appropriate ritual in these matters and that elaborate manuals of etiquette were not peculiar to the *bourgeois gentilshommes* of the Victorian era. There still survive such treatises of various countries and dates, and these confronted with miniatures, engravings and genre paintings can be made to yield up no small amount of information. Pictures and prints alone convey a good deal. Note for instance how at table the head of the family, and most gentlemen will sit in hat and cloak. In all but the most formal dances the gentlemen discard their cloaks while retaining their hats, for in polite society the hat often plays a part of its own in these salutatory exercises.

These may seem insignificant trifles, and indeed, if they are so to speak heavily underlined by the producer (who is after all ultimately responsible for seeing to it that a true *balance* is kept), they will simply look unreal and possibly absurd. Exaggeration may be justified in an empty fop or a parvenu —Lebeau, Osric, Parolles, Thurio and their like—but a Hamlet, a Mercutio, a Valentine must be schooled to carry off these little formalities lightly " as if to the manner born ".

Lovers of Dickens will remember the reference in *Nicholas Nickleby* to the over zealous actor who " blacked himself all over " to play the part of Othello. This has often been quoted since as an example of glorious absurdity, of histrionics gone mad. But is it ? Before the war there was a Shakespearian actor who ran that Dickensian barnstormer very close in his make-up for the part. He played it as a full-blooded negro and as his costume revealed a considerable portion of his anatomy he made no bones about blacking a good two-thirds of his person. Two large hip-baths would be filled with hot water in his dressing-room in readiness for the fall of the curtain.

For the actress bred up to trousers and mini-skirts worn with a minimum of underclothing, much adaptability is required to manœuvre gracefully and correctly in a farthingale and gown.

The famous French romantic actor (and talented sculptor), Mélingue, was likewise a champion of realism in details. Being cast for the part of " Don César de Bazan "—in Victor Hugo's *Ruy Blas*—he at once designed himself an elegant court-suit, which he had carried out in sumptuous materials. This he took home and dragged up and down through the thornbushes in his garden, finally leaving it exposed to sun, wind, rain and the birds of the air for some weeks. Having roughly cleaned it in time for the dress-rehearsal, he appeared in it, when the house rose at him on his entrance. A famous artist who witnessed it assured me that the effect was magical : the battle was won before Don César had opened his mouth. You knew him for a grandee degraded to the gutter. However modern techniques and treatments of textile fabrics, especially for screen and television productions, can achieve equally good results with considerably less effort !

The late Sir Henry Irving again, so I have been assured by those associated with his productions, had a rooted conviction of the importance of first impressions on the spectators' eye. He maintained that once an initial effect has been produced on the spectator it is apt to colour all that follows.

PLATE 6

Bodice with square décolletage filled in by a partlet, left open in the middle; puffed sleeves, short pointed waist; lace, closed ruff; ruffles; jewelled head ornament with diaphanous head-rail. *c.* 1578–80.

Queen Elizabeth I: unknown artist.
National Portrait Gallery, London.

It was thus that in *Madame Sans Gene* he was careful, when first " discovered " in the rôle of Napoleon, by ingenious *mise en scène* to create the impression of a relatively short, stout man. No man better realized the value of " holding the stage " or knew better how to do it.

Irving possessed in a marked degree the faculty of making costume and " props " significant : witness the carefully rehearsed " business " with Cardinal Wolsey's scarlet train in the first scene of *Henry VIII.*[1] Oftener than not, the appropriate period setting, if rightly apprehended, is not a hindrance but a help. But for this to be so designer, costumier, producer —*and actor* must understand their material and work in harmony to achieve a perfect whole. Miss X must be made to realize that the production is not designed primarily to show off her handsome shoulders and Mr Y that playing Shakespeare has *per se* no connection with " giving the girls a treat ".

It should be realized that nowadays the images of the past that the " man in the street " carries in his mind are in the main inspired by " the pictures " and the " telly ", and here it is that he is in a fair way to become the victim of more or less witting falsifiers of history. Directors, to whom the subject is possibly a closed book will rarely leave details of setting to the " expert " whom they have hired at much expense (presumably) to guarantee them from serious error. And in the matter of period there occur some " histori-cal " items blatantly false in details. In the early 1960s a television play set in the year of Waterloo had the cast playing croquet in one scene, and in 1973 a character of 1666 was shown smoking what appeared to be a briar pipe with a vulcanite mouthpiece.[2]

Speaking of pipes one must beware of modern "clays" with coloured varnished mouthpieces, introduced in the middle of the last century. In screen and television close ups these are sufficient to let down a scene that is authentic in all other respects. Although smoking is not mentioned in the Plays, it was certainly established by the 1570s.

It is not realized by the outside public under what handicaps the best qualified of designers is apt to labour. Nine times out of ten he is paid merely to let his name—which nine-tenths of the audience never notice and the remainder immediately forget (unless he happens to be the fashion

[1] With this may be compared Sarah Bernhardt's dramatic use of *her* train at the climax of *La Tosca*, and Moscowitch's ghastly removal of his rings as Shylock in the Trial Scene.

[2] On the other hand one can only praise the BBC's superb dressing of The Forsyte Saga, and of the Henry VIII and Elizabeth I series, in all of which great discernment was needed to detect the occasional " false quantity ".

of the moment)—appear on programme or screen. For the rest, so soon as he makes any effort to assert himself, he is sharply reminded that he is there simply as one " yes-man " more : soon he cynically resigns himself to take the cash and let the credit go. He soon learns that so far from being able to rely on loyal and intelligent co-operation, he must expect every man's hand to be against him.

As one who can claim an almost life-long acquaintance with the ways of the stage, I have no hesitation in saying that for the designer to tackle this job properly there are certain things he is entitled to find ready prepared for him before he sets pencil to paper. He should be furnished with at least a detailed scenario of the story, with all the proposed " business " contemplated ; a rough inventory of every change of dress and the " hand-props " required ; and the proposed cast with their individual characteristics. Moreover, his word should be final in all that concerns his special department and there should be no gerrymandering behind his back.

As an example of what may occur where the costume designer is not in possession of the necessary data, I may instance a production of *Bonny Dundee* in the West End, in which Claverhouse and his officers charged down the pass of Killiecrankie in the identical satin breeches and pumps in which we had just seen them at a court-ball.

The go-ahead manager and the diehard actor always fall back on a line of well-worn entrenchments.

1. It is impossible for period costume to be correct.

2. Even if it were, it would not be practical politics.

3. If these objections are scouted, there remains the probability that accuracy will be hailed by the public with derision.

In the first place it is perfectly possible for every one of Shakespeare's plays to be costumed in absolute concordance with a given period of history. Whether this is advisable in every case is another question, to which we revert in its proper place. Moreover it should be obvious that, as make-believe is the very breath of the theatre, we are not so foolish as to demand literal authenticity ; what we do insist upon is that what is exhibited should *seem* genuine. A realistic situation should be convincing in all its accidentals. Nowadays when every popular paper purports to let its readers see just how the wheels go round, you will hardly convince a modern crowd by childish conventions such as satisfy a Chinese audience. At any rate there is little difficulty in costuming any of the plays in such a way as to give a most satisfying impression of reality.

Given the requisite means of carrying out such an object, there is nothing fundamentally unpractical in faithfully doing so in a general way. All the objections usually brought against it rest on imperfect understanding, self-conscious timidity or unreasoning obstinacy. At every period fashion has been apt, in extreme cases, to degenerate into absurdity. But it is possible in practically every case to retain all the essential features, without stressing the exaggerations, which may on the other hand enhance the effect of the comic characters. Mediaeval and Renaissance costumes in the hands of a really intelligent tailor need not involve any serious discomfort to the wearer, though it is true that a rooted self-consciousness is a formidable barrier to the wearing in action of anything out of the common.

And thirdly—it will, I think, be found that for ridicule on the part of the audience the blame as often as not rests " behind " (that is to say with those actually concerned with the production); whether from imperfect performance, incomplete rehearsal or unforeseen accidents. Where none of these are present, the odds are that the audience will be favourably inclined. Have they not the wish to be entertained? And so long as they laugh not *at* but *with* the actor, why, that is all to the good.

If it were necessary to appeal to evidence, we cannot do better than to cite that delightful French film *La Kermesse héroïque* which ran uninterruptedly in the West End for seven months in the 1930's.[1] This apparently started with the advantages which I postulated at the outset as indispensable for success to every play or film, irrespective of time or place: a good, straightforward story, admirable craftmanship and first-rate acting: Mme Françoise Rosay's rendering of the burgomaster's wife in particular remains a precious memory. One went and went again, and sent all one's friends who in turn sent theirs. I have, as far back as I can remember, witnessed plays and films, including outstanding successes, in England, France and Germany, and I do not hesitate to say that I have never seen more artistic care expended on bringing to life a definite historic epoch: in this case the Spanish Netherlands of the early 17th century. The pains lavished over every detail of costume and setting, the intelligence, taste and research evident throughout played no little part in its success. Far from distracting one from the interest of the comedy, so perfectly were they wedded to the situation that they seemed to lend added zest to every point.

[1] And has recently (1973) been revived by the BBC for television.

The Flemish burghers and their wives might have stepped straight out of canvases by Frans Hals, de Keyser or Mytens. Even from the point of view of the cheapest seats the " shots " in which Mme Rosay puts on her verdingale and best velvet gown were of undeniable entertainment value.

The march too of the Spanish envoy and his military train through the streets of Boom was a perfect piece of production.

Fighting occupies a great deal of room in the Shakespearian drama. It is consequently unfortunate that whether in single combat or in pitched battle there is still difficulty in achieving any very convincing pictures. The general result is fidgety and confused rather than arresting. I speak particularly of hand-to-hand fighting. The average man does not even know how to hold a sword or a dagger, let alone how to use them. In combat the right forefinger should be crossed over the *quillons* (= cross-bar) of the sword and the left thumb laid flat upon the dagger-blade at its junction with the hilt. Indeed by all races who practise fighting with dagger or knife, the weapon is held blade upward like a whip, not downward like an oar. Women instinctively grasp a sword-hilt close to the pummel, instead of gripping it next to the blade. When it comes to a duel, other than with pistols, the average actor belongs to one of two types : the nervous or the reckless. Both are unfit to be entrusted with a sword. Even for stage-purposes a fencer is not made overnight : and whether on the stage or on the screen an assault at arms is apt to be a sad disappointment. Comparatively few Shakespearian actors of any experience can claim to have come through unscathed. Rapier-play is deadliest of all on account of the constant risk to the combatants' eyes. Perhaps the most thrilling duel I ever saw was with rapier and dagger in Oscar Asche's production of *Count Hannibal*. It lasted about one minute and a half[1] and was always one of the " high spots " of the performance. Yet, one night during the Australian run, Asche's opponent was within a hair's breadth of losing an eye and ended the encounter with the blood dripping from his face ! Most telling no doubt, and the luckless actor brought down the house ; but decidedly not a triumph to be repeated. It is for this reason that the producer in despair is driven to fall back on meaningless capers ; as in the many instances where the combatants—for no obvious reason—fight out their duel up and down a staircase, calling up memories of the waltz in *The Merry Widow*. In all cases the

[1] A short time the reader may suppose. As one who has had to time the movements in a ballet, let me assure him that, when properly planned, a good deal of " business " can be transacted in a minute and a half.

assistance of a competent " fight arranger " should be employed for professional productions.

If actual duels and mass attacks are rarely very convincing, the actual preliminaries, troops on the march and on parade, etc., might well be a good deal more realistic than we usually see them. The England of Shakespeare's day happens to be rich in military treatises, from which we can learn in detail all the particulars of arming, drill and manœuvres, the relative position of the various troops, and the correct deportment of officers and men alike. In the London of our own day Trooping the Colour, the changing of the Guard and similar military rites seldom fail to draw a crowd. It is hard to believe that such spectacles as an old-time army marching out to war or returning in triumph could not be so produced on stage or (especially) screen as to give the spectator a thrill. I can remember a performance of *Faust* at the Brussels opera house (Théâtre de la Monnaie) in which the producer had seemingly been given *carte blanche* to let himself go over the " Soldier's Chorus ", with the result that the house too " let *it*self go " in thunders of applause. It was well and truly earned, for he had expended both trouble and imagination over his effect. In all military groupings muskets should be carefully differentiated from arquebuses (calivers). The latter are light, with curved stocks and are discharged from the left breast ; the former cumbrous, with straight stock and fired from the right shoulder, for which purpose they require to be propped on a forked *rest*.[1] Most muskets are matchlocks ; calivers often wheel-locks. The tactics of a troop of pikes in their hedgehog-like formation, whether receiving cavalry or advancing to the attack, seem to offer good material for a historical film. The march-past of troops is a feature of *Troilus and Cressida, Corolianus, All's well that ends well,* etc., that could be made immensely effective on the screen.

A warning that every director of productions on stage and screen cannot take too early to heart is against the lavish and indiscriminate use of arms and armour in scenes of every-day life. Even knights and soldiers generally did not go about their more humdrum occupations, " armed at all points ", and the popular conception of them as men whose waking hours were normally spent locked from top to toe in shining steel is only worthy of Wardour Street. And here I will venture to quote from Miss Dorothy Hartley's *Mediæval Costume and Life* (Batsford 1931).

[1] Each must be accompanied by its appropriate " furniture " : bandoleers, powder-flask, touch-box, etc.

"Even the heaviest-armed cavalry—the 'men at arms' as they were termed from the 15th century—only wore *cap à pié* armour on special occasions or when immediate fighting was expected; in fact the helmet and gauntlets were rarely donned except on the very point of charging into action. Armour at best was never *comfortable*, and only cowardice or childish vanity can normally have induced a man to encase himself wholly in a steel shell for any longer than mere expediency dictated. . . . Contrary to 'romantic' conceptions, gentlemen *previous to the 16th century* did not normally wear swords. The only weapon that is normally in evidence —from the early 14th century onward—with civilian apparel is the dagger. In an unruly and imperfectly policed age, the authorities, ever suspicious of armed risings, sternly discouraged the bearing of other lethal weapons by all classes without valid reasons. Thus in troubled times travellers might carry a sword or other arm against emergencies on the road. . . . Both mail and (later) plate necessitated the use of special underwear. . . . It must be remembered . . . that the donning and adjustment of the complete fighting-kit, even with every item laid in readiness and help at hand, took from first to last a good deal of time, nor was the task of disarming much easier. Yet I have read a story of a fugitive, with the hunt at his very heels, baffling the pursuers by concealing himself at a moment's notice in one of the panoplies in the 'ancestral' armoury. Not time only but practice was required for the proper adjustment of the numerous ties, buckles and catches which held the equipment in position." While it is nowise essential for stage armour to be as heavy as the real thing it must not be manifestly so light as to kill illusion. For the same reason, where mail of silvered string is employed, it becomes necessary to weight the free edges with a light jack chain or other device. On the other hand hoods of mail, where made of metal, require a padded under cap to save the scalp from chafing.

Note that the sword and sheath could be discarded simply by unhooking the hangers (Fig. 45). It was not unusual for a duellist to bare his sword by giving his *sheathed* weapon a sharp flourish, which sent scabbard and hangers flying. A none too scrupulous swordsman would so direct their flight as to strike his enemy in the face. By Shakespeare's time the good old-fashioned English sword and buckler were accounted altogether plebeian: in Florio's view (*First Frutes . . .*, etc., 1578) "clownish, dastardly weapons and not for a gentleman". In stage-duels rapier and dagger are almost always fought with weapons of the too familiar cuphilted variety. The only excuse for them is the protection they afford the fencers' hands. Actually they are quite inappropriate because (1) they were unknown till well into the 17th century (2) they are of rare occurrence outside Spain and Italy.

45. Swordsman. Hangers detached from girdle; scabbard about to be dropped; full trunkhose with canions; garters and shoe roses; copotain hat. *c.* 1611.
The Maids Tragedy, Beaumont and Fletcher. Woodcut in British Museum.

It is clearly impossible in a work on this scale to give comprehensive or even general instructions upon the correct use of costume and its accessories. One can but hope that the rather random suggestions made in this chapter may prove fruitful and lead the reader to think out further points for himself. Let us repeat once more that what is urged here is not reality but the *illusion* of reality. Above all the appearance of historical accuracy should never seem an expensive extra, should never be allowed to distract attention from the central theme, but employed rather to underline its verisimilitude by blending with it as a natural accompaniment.

For a fuller discussion on the wearing of historic clothes for the stage, including descriptions of contemporary manners and techniques I can recommend Ruth Green's *The Wearing of Costume*.

A final warning. The most perfect of settings will go for nothing if the actor refuses to make up in accordance with time and place—*and subject*.

Equally important is the question of a correct coiffure for both men and women.

It is amazing how often one sees an otherwise good costume effect spoilt by being crowned with a modern " hair-do ". As far as the ladies are concerned this seems to have been a recurrent fault at all periods : whatever costume the 18th and 19th centuries attempted, as well as the 20th, nearly always the actresses portrayed in contemporary illustrations are wearing the hair styles of their own day.

If a sergeant-major is keenly alive to the smallest example of " improper dressing ", why cannot the experienced actor realize the telling effect of correct " costume " correctly used ? For my part I cannot understand anyone deliberately selecting an historical subject and then jibbing at its implications. If choose it you must, be as careful of the appropriate setting and " properties " as you would be in a modern film to get the details of an aeroplane, a motor-car or a telephone as " right " as possible. Why propagate errors in the one more than the other ?

CHAPTER VI

THE PLAYS

I. THE HISTORIES

It is usual in modern copies of the *Complete Works* to find the " Tragedies ", " Comedies " and " Histories " arranged in three separate groups. The last-named commonly comprise only the subjects borrowed from English chronicles from *King John* to *Henry VIII*. But one can hardly deny the claim of *Richard III* to be a tragedy, any more than that of *Antony and Cleopatra* to rank as history. Certainly from the designer's point of view the Roman dramas—*Coriolanus, Julius Caesar* and *Antony and Cleopatra*—would seem to demand an emphasis on the historical element. *Titus Andronicus* might perhaps be grouped with these, if it were at all possible to take that bloodthirsty fustian seriously. Of the Greek subjects the only one that to me invites a realistic setting is *Timon*. *Troilus and Cressida*, that cynical tragi-comedy, was once very effectively presented at Stratford-on-Avon in a setting of (about) 1580, rather in the French style than after the Spanish or Italian pattern. *Pericles* also, but for the names, has little or nothing of the Hellenic spirit, and does not in fact fit very well into any class. But these are all plays of very doubtful importance, and are performed, if at all, rather *pour mémoire*. I do not propose, therefore, to dwell further upon general questions of setting. Those I *am* including in my list follow in chronological order of subject.

TIMON OF ATHENS

Although *Timon* has never been a favourite and is very rarely " put on ", it strikes me as in its way a deeply moving play and less improbable than most critics will allow. Also it seems to me to lend itself with some plausibility to a genuine ancient Greek setting, which is an opportunity for beautiful pictures combined with simplicity. No setting calls for less extravagance and finer taste. In theory—if we take no account of armour—no costume should be easier to reproduce, being nothing more than simple drapery. Neither costly materials nor skilled tailoring are demanded. Unlike the characteristic Roman wardrobe, that of the Greeks of classic times is wholly composed of rectangular pieces of stuff, folded and draped on the person. In practice it is rare to find the effect aimed at successfully realized. The ready made tunics and cloaks supplied by theatrical costumiers almost always look mean and shabby. There is no such thing as " fit " : you must learn to estimate the dimensions of the pieces required in each case, and, for a satisfactory result, the material (even if eventually secured by tacks and pins) must first be draped on the living model. Any of the standard reference-books on classical dress or antiquities will serve to get the general notion : Smith's Dictionary of *Greek and Roman Antiquities*, Guhl and Koner, Saglio and Daremberg. Further you may consult Lucy Barton's book, and, for the correct draping, Mary Houston, Margarete Bieber, Margot Lister and—best of all—Léon Heuzey's *Histoire du Costume Antique*. But first and last study the antique itself.

CORIOLANUS. JULIUS CAESAR. ANTONY AND CLEOPATRA

There is no such thing as a *history* of Roman costume, for the very good reason that no evidence worth speaking of, whether literary or pictorial, has as yet been collected to trace its evolution from an earlier date than the close of the Republic. So far as arms and armour alone are concerned, a systematic attempt to compile something of the sort has been made by Couissin, and in a more romantic, picturesque spirit we have Forestier's rather sketchy *The Roman Soldier*. More up to date is Graham Webster's *Roman Army*. How to stage *Coriolanus* in accordance with its traditional date remains something of a problem. But for *Julius Caesar* and for the Roman characters in *Antony and Cleopatra* the same wardrobe will serve, since but a few years divide them chronologically. Cleopatra, it should be remembered, was almost entirely Greek in culture, and the Egyptian note in her apparel should not be emphasized. As in all Roman plays, the make and draping of the *toga* is the test. The stage toga is generally much too skimpy and the effect of the garment is thereby lost. Generally speaking, to achieve the right effect a minimum length of between two and a half and three times the wearer's height is needed—for a 6-foot man from 15 to 18 feet—and the width should be between 6 and 9 feet, also according to height, at the widest part. The cut is a segment of a circle. If decorated, the band of red, blue or purple should be along the length of the straight side.

Tunics also suffer from skimpiness—for men and women they should be ankle length and shoulder width, drawn in at the waist by a girdle. Workmen's and military tunics, however, were " mini " length, to, or above, the knee, and sometimes shaped to the waist.

Cloaks, a military fashion, capes, etc., should all be adequate in size and cut.

The toga was made of wool ; outer garments of wool also. Tunics might be wool or linen.

The female equivalent of the toga was the stola, similar in size but cut straight, not as an arc.

Colours were varied—tunics of reds, terra cotta, browns, yellows, greens. The military cloak is well in scarlet or crimson. Togas, generally, were white.

See Heuzey's chapter in his *Costume Antique*, Kohler and Lister. All three plays seem to demand exact adherence to period in *mise en scène* and this is perfectly feasible—at least of the two last.

KING JOHN

Mediaeval costume about this date is at its most graceful and least eccentric. No specially clever tailoring is required to achieve a convincing effect. Practically all the armour for the better class warriors consists of *mail* (i.e. a network of interlinked rings commonly mis-named " chain armour ", see p. 72).

The imitation mail of thick plaited string can be fairly realistic if the silvering is artfully done and all free edges weighted by sewing a thin jack-chain along them to convey the drag of the real thing. The hood attached to the *hauberk* (coat of mail) should be cut and adapted to the head (when worn) as shown in Fairholt, Vol. I, figs. 105, 106, or Kelly and Schwabe, *Short History*, Vol. I, fig. 33. Otherwise, unless the hood fits *perfectly*, it will betray itself as the fake it is. It is worth while to stress again two points : (*a*) the head and hands should not be armed except for actual battle ; and (*b*) *where the face is not clean-shaven*, the moustache is practically always accompanied by more or less beard. This holds good of all the " Histories " from *King John* to *Henry VIII* : no beard, no moustache. From *c*. 1420 to 1520 the general rule is neither.

RICHARD II. HENRY IV. HENRY V. HENRY VI (I)

These are here grouped together because of certain general characteristics of fashion common to the whole period they cover, especially as regards male attire. Costume from now on grows increasingly fantastic. In fact, the period from the reign of Richard II to the end of the Wars of the Roses includes some of the oddest freaks of fashion of the whole Middle Ages. While for practical considerations it is imperative in most cases to modify certain details, it is no less desirable to preserve the distinctive character throughout and above all to avoid introducing an alien note.

> For a satisfying effect a correct cut is of first importance. As regards masculine apparel by far the most useful work ever published—within its express limitations—is Adrien Harmand's *Jeanne d'Arc: Ses Costumes, son Armure*. In its special line no more exhaustive study exists. While it is primarily a close enquiry into the clothing and armour affected by Joan of Arc and her male contemporaries, to read it with close attention is to learn the basic principles of male costume 1400–40. When published it revealed a number of details hitherto unsuspected by costume-students. The numerous tailor's patterns—hardly a variant type is omitted—have been cut out and made up to the last stitch and button by the author himself from contemporary evidence. Their practical accuracy and convincing effect have been rigorously tested on the living model in action : throughout they proved in all respects thoroughly satisfying.

HENRY VI (II, III). RICHARD III

Note that after 1450 there is a distinct change in the fashions. Armour (of the type miscalled " Gothic ") is at its zenith of perfection, especially in the last quarter of the century. No sort of makeshift will serve to give its picturesque effect on the stage. It is worth pointing out that the steeple-shaped " hennin " is scarcely seen on lady's heads till towards 1460 ; for amateurs *will* drag it into " mediaeval " costume indiscriminately. Moreover, it was characteristic of France and Burgundy rather than England, where, when worn, it was of a truncated pattern.

(The best of books on mediaeval costume is undoubtedly the Cunningtons' *Handbook*.)

HENRY VIII

Here you have the advantage of the portraits by Holbein and what is rather loosely called his " school " for the principal characters introduced.

However much the rest of the cast may formerly have taken the boards apparelled in the style of the actors' own period, there seems at all dates to have been a conscientious attempt to reproduce Holbein's picture of the king, and also (in a minor degree) to suggest the personality of Wolsey. Do *not* make a wholesale parade of "crested" (=fluted) armour, which is characteristic rather of Germany and—in a measure—Italy.[1] Brasses and (especially) sepulchral effigies are your best models, since actual *English* armour of the early 16th century is practically non-existent. There is no occasion for armour anyhow.

II. THE TRAGEDIES

It is probably the tragedies which are apt to provoke most differences of opinion as regards their setting. For such of my readers as pin their faith to the style of production represented by Reinhardt and Komisarjevsky any suggestions of mine are likely to be worse than useless. Though I should henceforth stand condemned as hopelessly unprogressive, let me confess that the modern German-Russian school leaves me cold; of them all Bakst alone stirs me to admiration. Not the most elaborate production of Shakespeare at His Majesty's Theatre before the war[2] distracted me more from the true object of the play than does the ostentatious austerity of these "modern" shows. They are to me merely fidgety. As for the "close-ups" so admired by film directors, I can never see one without immediately recalling those huge Oxo posters that made hideous our hoardings.

CYMBELINE

I cannot quite feel that this play fits naturally into tragedy, comedy or tragi-comedy. To me it always reads curiously like certain of the old-fashioned fairy tales collected by the Brothers Grimm, from which the fairies, witches and ogres have been carefully eliminated. The actual story never seems to strike a note of realism. Imogen is the only character that lives, but her adventures in the cave with Belarius and her brothers

[1] Cf. Sir J. Mann: *Notes on the armour of the Maximilian period and the Italian wars* (*Archaeologia* LXXIX—1929—pp. 217–224).

[2] I.e. 1914.

have a smack of the tale of the "Three Bears". The play seems to call for such "Britons" and "Romans" as are engraved in old-time chronicles and maps of England. The Renaissance conception of Britons, Romans, Danes, Saxons and Normans is more in harmony with the tone of the play than any attempt at historical truth; and allows of unlimited freedom of treatment.

46. Sexton of Peterborough Cathedral; old-fashioned long-skirted sleeved jerkin worn open; trunkhose, shoes with large roses; black skull cap; dog whip. *c.*1590. Portrait of Robert Scarlett. Peterborough Cathedral.

HAMLET

Where this has not been produced in a purely fanciful spirit, efforts have been made to reproduce something of the Viking age. I do not feel that these are ever quite successful. While I cannot reconcile myself to a 20th-century *mise en scène*, I do feel that the play fits in very well with a period not too remote from its original production; in fact not much earlier than the middle of the 16th century. Moreover, there are a number of passages in the text, some of them too important to be slurred over, which are hardly in keeping with an earlier date: "armed from head to foot"—"he wore his *beaver* up"—"a pair of provincial *roses*"—"*rapier and dagger*"—"the carriages . . . are the *hangers*", etc.

The all-important business of the change of "foils" in the last act is wholly at variance with the modern *épée* play so frequently introduced on the stage. The term "carriages" for *hangers* may be a euphemism: at all events I know no other instance of it, and to Hamlet himself, it was evidently unfamiliar. It is by no means clear that Laertes actually challenges Hamlet *to a match with rapier and dagger.* These are merely mentioned as his stakes (against six Barbary horses) and the weapons in which he had great skill. "Foils" only are named in the assault-at-arms. Cup-hilt rapiers in any case suit neither time nor place. The fencing bout requires most judicious planning and rehearsal. M. Paul Dubois of the Paris Opera published a detailed study of this particular fight, but used cup-hilted rapiers and correspondent daggers.

A nice 16th-century grave digger is to be seen at Peterborough (Fig. 46).

KING LEAR

To me *King Lear* has nothing of the romantic Britain one finds in *Cymbeline*. Rather does it suggest the period of the Arthurian cycle as developed in the 11th and 12th centuries. Not that it can be described in the main as reflecting the so-called " age of chivalry ", but there are touches in the play that accord with it, and the *mise en scène* of that period seems in many ways better adapted to the action of the play than a remote age of dolmens and bronze celts. A primitive pre-Christian presentation, if consistently realized, is apt to verge on the pedantic. Something carried out in the spirit of the late Edwin Austin Abbey's " Grail " series would on the other hand lend itself well enough to the character of the story, rather than any rigidly historical scenes. On the other hand the actual *decorations* might, without jarring unduly, be kept on a Celtic note, while the *shapes* might recall the "early English" period. The scenes on the heath, during the storm, etc., can moreover be designed to suggest throughout an echo of a more primaeval age. Much tact is required to strike a happy medium. Thus the duel between Edgar and Edmund is conceived in the true mediaeval spirit, and in at least one case this was the least successful feature of an otherwise beautiful production.

MACBETH

Here we have more or less historic data for a starting-point, to which a touch of realism is lent by the mention of Edward the Confessor and the introduction of his general Siward. The date being thus fixed shortly before the Norman Conquest, it is no great matter to present this tragedy in the trappings of a period at once suitable and highly picturesque, without doing violence to it from any point of view. There are no stage directions of any kind likely to hamper the business of the producer. Yet *Macbeth* is far more easily imagined as contemporary with Edward the Confessor than with Elizabeth or James I, whatever may have been the practice at the Globe Theatre. (Here the Bayeaux Tapestry will prove a useful guide.)

OTHELLO

Rightly or wrongly, I have always pictured this play as an Elizabethan story. Apart from this, one feels that to Europe at large Cyprus and Famagusta were imperishably linked with the Turkish war that ended in their capture by the Turks in 1570, in particular with the last stand of Bragadino and Baglione against Mustapha. These were the type of warriors popularly associated with the island and with its defence. The fighters that sailed with Othello will be no doubt best modelled on those, largely Venetian, that fought at Lepanto.

A point which has given rise to more controversy than all the rest is the correct dress and make-up of the hero. If we will only divest ourselves of romantic notions of " the noble Moor ", we shall make no bones about admitting that a *Negro in European clothing and armour* alone fits the bill. The tawny, turbaned " Moor " armed like Boabdil, dear to Victorian sentimentalists, would to Elizabethans have been indistinguishable from " circumcised dogs ",[1] like Mustapha and Ali Pasha, against whom he was fighting. The late Oscar Asche, though he insisted on dressing Othello as an Oriental, yet made him up as a full-blooded Negro. Only a rooted prejudice against " colour " could lead an audience to deny his dignified appearance and bearing in the part, which was one of his outstanding successes. Mr Paul Robeson, on the other hand, has played the part dressed as a European, and if his actual performance fell short of expectations, no critic could find fault with him on that score. It was precisely the turban and tawny skin of the Turk and Barbary-Moor that to Shakespeare's age heralded death to Christian men. The *true Negro* was merely unfamiliar and quaint.

> There is a piece of evidence in my favour which, so far as I am aware, has passed unnoted by critics and actors alike. In 1608 Alvaro, fourth Christian King of Congo, despatched one of his subjects as ambassador to the Pope, by whom he was received with signal honour as a valued guest. Falling ill in a short while, he was personally blessed on his death-bed, and his body deposited under an escort of the Swiss Guard in Sta Maria Maggiore. The event was of sufficient interest for Lucas Kilian, the German engraver, to publish a print of the circumstance, with a bust of the envoy, Antonio Manoel de Vunth, apparently *in*

[1] Do not forget that these are Christian Othello's *own* scornful words of " a turbaned Turk ".

PLATE 7

Jacket of linen embroidered with black silk, slightly flared below waist, fitting sleeves with broad flat wings, no collar. Skirt (kirtle) similar, but differing pattern. *c.* 1610.

London Museum, Kensington Palace, London.

the Italian costume of the period. The inscription refers to the contrast with *this Negro's native attire.*

The play, more particularly with the resources of the screen, lends itself to various novel effects : e.g. the flagship with its three lanterns on the poop. Cassio's "coat", when he is ambushed by Roderigo and Iago in the night, should be clearly seen to be a brigandine or other obvious vesture of defence, concealed beneath his cloak till he exclaims: "That thrust had been mine enemy indeed but that my coat is better than thou think'st".

Although it does not directly concern costume or properties, I cannot refrain from citing as particularly effective the arrangement of the " council chamber " scene in the Berlin production. For some reason this is apt to be treated as an occasion for pomp and display. Othello makes something of state-entry, and harangues a more or less crowded senate, standing while they sit, as it were, in formal judgment ; none of which seems to harmonize with the text. Very different was the staging in Berlin with Bassermann in the name-part. Here was indeed an intimate council, called " haste post haste " in sharp emergency. The Duke and half a dozen senators are seated by candlelight at a table covered with despatches on a dais. The lighting is concentrated on this group, Othello's and Brabantio's few followers take their station on either side in front in dim half-light. The Moor on entering is at once beckoned to a seat at the council-board and plays his whole scene seated there quite naturally. The whole effect was " private and confidential "—and urgent.

ROMEO AND JULIET

For some reason it seems usual to imagine this drama in a guise modelled on Venetian paintings by Carpaccio and Pintoricchio[1]. At that, the younger men are apt to be decked with moustaches and " Vandyke " beards (reminiscent of La Scala and Covent Garden Opera) that are at hopeless variance with the costume. Indeed the whole thing generally smacks of grand opera rather than of " straight drama ". There is, however, no particular objection to the choice of this period, except (1) that it is not really consistent with the lavish use of swords, still less with the school of fencing for which Mercutio derides Tybalt ; (2) it has been served up to us to repletion. If

[1] I.e. of the late 15th and early 16th centuries.

we decide to disregard the first objection—and it can at a pinch be toned down—I would suggest at any rate that we might have a change from the eternal figures of Gounod's *Roméo et Juliette,* and try something more akin to the traditional period of the story, the 14th century. There are a number of North Italian paintings, frescos and illuminated MSS. which have as yet been not at all exploited, yet are rich in material. I would note in particular the frescos at the castle of Manta (Piedmont), in the Popes' Palace at Avignon and—best of all—a wonderful *Veronese* picture-book now in the Kunsthistorisches Museum at Vienna.[1] The Italy of the Middle Ages does exist, after all, outside of Carpaccio's paintings, and it is time producers of *Romeo and Juliet* remembered it.

On the other hand there seems no valid obstacle, when all is said and done, to setting this piece in an Elizabethan or at any rate 16th-century setting. Italian costume of, say, 1540 to 1550 lends itself to most attractive treatment, besides having the advantage of being in harmony with the spirit of the poet's age. The contemporary duellists' swaggering trick of shaking the sheathed sword free with a flick of the wrist is the kind of thing to commend itself to " the furious Tybalt ", and Romeo can walk at ease in his " French slop ". The duel by the way seems, as described by Benvolio, to have been a rapier-and-dagger contest.

It should be remembered that Tybalt is an avowed swashbuckler, and it is clear that in the duel scene he is abroad in Verona's streets " looking for trouble " with Romeo. Therefore he may fitly appear in brigandine and mail-sleeves, with sword and dagger ; Mercutio, otherwise unarmed, may, being kinsman to the prince, have his sword carried after him by a page ; while Romeo, a temporary pacifist, may well be without weapons. Then, infuriated by Mercutio's death by a foul blow—" I was hurt under your arm "—he can pick up his friend's sword to avenge him. This has been done and, neatly managed, is obviously good " business ".

III. THE COMEDIES

Of these a number seem without effort to lend themselves to the costume of the poet's day. These, therefore, it may be as well to approach without more ado.

[1] *Jahrbuch der kunsthistorischen Sammlungen*, etc., Vienna. A remarkable panorama of life in ancient Verona. Vol. XVI (1895), pp. 144–230.

ALL'S WELL THAT ENDS WELL

Indifferent as this play is, it has the negative virtue of lending itself admirably to picturesque stage-pictures. There is no particular reason why the " King of France " should not be made up from an individual monarch : Henri II, III or IV, as he is not made to take a personal share in the Italian wars. Although the scene is " partly in Tuscany ", practically the whole cast, excepting " Diana " and her mother and friends, is French. Historically perhaps Henri II would best fit the story, though for variety of costume Henri IV gives more scope. The various camp-scenes and especially the march past of the troops in Act III, Sc. 5, offer fine opportunities. Parolles in particular is a part which allows the extravagances of contemporary fashion to be emphasized without restraint.

LOVE'S LABOUR'S LOST

Another piece that almost exacts an Elizabethan colouring. No distinction should be attempted between the " King of Navarre's " followers and the suite of the " Princess of France ". I have seen an attempt made to clothe this comedy in 15th-century garb. Nothing seemed to me to be gained by this, and Don Adriano's effect was nil. The " fantastical Spaniard " only tells in his surroundings when attired as a caricature of the Dons that sailed with the Armada : towering bag-shaped cap, huge ruff, short cape with a hood, trunkhose of exaggerated width and shoes slashed across, his dress should be black throughout. The " Muscovites " should not be over-realistic ; as for the " Worthies " they are of course caricatures of the parts, but should not seem too deliberately so.

MUCH ADO ABOUT NOTHING

It seems difficult to believe the *mise en scène* of this story is not in a measure inspired by the victory of Lepanto. It would be impossible in Shakespeare's day for any man at all conversant with the doings of the great world to hear Messina coupled with *Don John, the Prince's bastard brother*, without being reminded of the campaign of the Holy League. Don Pedro, Don John and Borachio—possibly too Leonato and his brother—may with perfect propriety be presented as Spaniards, and Conrade after the fashion of a German landsknecht. For that matter Benedick when attired as " a

German from the waist downwards, all slops ", may allowably be taken to have borrowed the fashion from the German mercenaries so numerous at that time in Continental armies. The play contains other passages relative to fashions. It is as well to utter a word of warning here with regard to the so-called landsknecht-fashions. There is a tendency in pieces designed in the Elizabethan-continental style to introduce German soldiers of the " Maximilian " type. Even worse was Beerbohm Tree's " Benedick " in the German-Swiss attire just mentioned. It was copied from a portrait of the first duke of Guise dated 1526 (i.e. a full generation earlier in style than those which surrounded him) and in no sense conveyed the explicit words of the text. The correct shape of the " slops " is shown in Figure 8.

47. Venice: Jewish girl in dress with elbow-length sleeves, gathered skirt, low-cut bodice with stomacher, and a neckerchief; long apron. 1601. Contemporary woodcut, *Eve of Yom Kippur*. Bodleian Library.

MERCHANT OF VENICE

In *Othello* we see little of everyday Venice. One gets in fact little more than a fleeting glimpse of it by night amid conditions of haste and anxiety before being whisked away to Cyprus in a state of war. In the *Merchant of Venice* we have every opportunity of showing the great sea-power with its government and commerce; for none of the comedies is in a sense so un-English. Here is little or nothing borrowed from the life with which Shakespeare was familiar. One is at liberty to reproduce the Venetian atmosphere to one's heart's content. Fortunately one has no lack of pictorial evidence to draw upon in dressing one's cast, whether of the author's own day or earlier. As Venice was perhaps the most cosmopolitan city of the Renaissance, great variety can be introduced into the crowds. Other notes are struck by the princes of Morocco and Aragon with their suites. As for Shylock there is nothing very novel to suggest concerning his appearance. Whether or not to depict him as a native Jew or a manifest Oriental seems to be chiefly a matter of taste. The turban, caftan and sash have at least the advantage of causing his figure to strike a note of contrast with his Christian opponents. There are lines in the text which suggest a man who lives in no great comfort, preferring to hoard his wealth rather than flaunt it in his opponents' eyes. Only his hatred of the gentiles can break through the ingrained love of hoarded gold : one would imagine him rather shabby in

48. Italian. Jewish woman in a gown and cloak; ruff, and ruffles at the wrists; reticulated caul with kerchief attached. (The ruff was retained by Jewish ladies long after it ceased to be universally worn.) 1602.
Etching "*Hebrea*", Rome, 1602. British Museum.

49. Italian. Jewish man wearing doublet and hose; small falling band; long cloak; on his head a *barrette*, a type of cap or beret associated with Jewish dress. He carries a handkerchief, and other garments. 1594.
Engraving, *Judaeus Mercator Palavinus*. Padua, 1594.

his attire. Tubal, not Shylock, would represent the Rothschilds of Jewry.
(See Figures 47, 48 and 49 for typical Italian Jewish dress.)

THE TAMING OF THE SHREW

In spite of the Italian names, an English rather than an Italian colouring seems indicated, especially if the "Induction" is retained. There are a number of references to costume in the text (equally applicable to England or Italy) to which producers rarely pay any attention, whether from ignorance of their meaning or sheer indifference. Petruchio's wedding attire and that of his servant Grumio are in a measure ready-made for you by Shakespeare, and nothing is gained by trying to be " quainter " than he. The stage-Petruchio is mostly a mere figure of fun and rarely succeeds in being credible to the eye. He should be clad not in a kind of fancy-dress but in *worn-out oddments* of contemporary fashion. The wares of the haberdasher and tailor moreover are worthy to be made a minor feature instead of being (as is usual) meaningless scraps of tawdry finery. They should be *exhibited* to best advantage.

TWELFTH NIGHT

" Illyria " here is obviously not a name of any special significance, and it is probably wasted ingenuity to make it an excuse for introducing an alleged " Dalmatian " element into the costumes. Viola, after all, is masquerading as " a young gentleman ", not as an Albanian chieftain. The whole business of the confusion between her and Sebastian is generally made not more probable, but less so, if we dress them up in any conspicuous habit ; for the essential likeness of their apparel—it need not be *perfectly* identical in detail—is wholly a coincidence. Only if they wear a plain, well-cut suit such as would not stand out from their surroundings, will the mistake pass muster. Likeliest of all would be an all-black costume of satin or velvet, modestly trimmed. It is the sort of costume that in Elizabeth's reign would be of frequent recurrence, being " good form " in almost any surroundings. It is also possible to introduce trifling differences hardly noticeable till brother and sister are confronted. At this time of day it should not be necessary to warn producers against the use by Malvolio of supposed " cross garters " in the style of the old-fashioned stage-brigand. We have explained the true use of the term elsewhere (and see Fig. 12). The humour of this point, such as it is, consists in cross-garters being distinctly *démodé* by the time the play was originally put on. Sir Toby is a gentleman run to seed and a parasite and should be dressed accordingly ; while Sir Andrew should be a clumsy copy of a man of fashion. In both the Elizabethan modes can be rather caricatured ; but Sir Andrew with a touch of the dapper, while Toby's clothes, ill-matched and slovenly, denote the confirmed sot.

MEASURE FOR MEASURE

To take the " Vienna " of this play seriously into consideration in considering its *mise en scène,* especially since most of the characters are Italians by their names, would hardly be a critical performance. As however it may as well be placed in German Europe as anywhere else, no objection can be made to taking advantage of its pretended scene to make a picturesque ensemble. There is nothing to hinder us from availing ourselves of the innumerable paintings and prints of the German school for the purpose (Fig. 50). There is, too, something in the fantastic variety of form and colour not out of harmony with the rather grim character of the story, in its rather brutish exuberance ; and the humours of the comic element fit well enough with the German modes of apparel of the first half of the 16th century. Dürer and his confrères supply a rare abundance of material upon which to draw.

50. German, gown with full, square sleeves, deep fur collar; bonnet with slashed brim. First half of 16th century.
After *A History of Costume,* Carl Köhler.

THE MERRY WIVES OF WINDSOR

To me the proper setting of this play—unless we decide to dress *all* the plays, " Histories " included, in Elizabethan garb—has always been an open question. My decided bias in favour of a strict adherence to period, at any rate in all the plays with a definite historical basis, should by this time be manifest. In the present instance the point at issue seems to me to be this : is Falstaff to be as to his outer man the personage we have met in *Henry IV* ? If so, I am in no two minds about it : the play must be cast in an early 15th-century setting throughout, for the one principle on which I would insist in the case of each and every play is consistency. There must be nothing that clashes with the general character. On the other hand none of the plays lends itself so readily to a purely Elizabethan frame. But if we decide to mount it accordingly, we must be resigned to forget Falstaff the boon-companion of Prince Hal and to picture him solely as a *vieux marcheur* of the 16th century, tippling and intriguing in half-timbered hostelries. And indeed the laughing philosopher of *Henry IV* has here declined to something nearer the level of Major Bagstock.

THE REMAINING COMEDIES

I find it difficult to associate any of these with such realism as is implied by any definite period. To any of them, greatly as they vary in point of merit, the suggestion of Rostand as to the fit setting of his fanciful comedy of *Les Romanesques* might in great measure be applied : any time and place that afford an opportunity of graceful costumes. Thus when *As you like it* was put on (with Miss Edith Evans) in a series of Watteauesque *fêtes galantes* I could not feel that the production was really alien in spirit to the theme of the play. Certainly Theseus, Hippolyta and the Athens of *The Midsummer Night's Dream* recall rather the mediaeval romance of *Theseis* or Chaucer's *Knight's Tale* than the memories of Greek legend. This fanciful note clings in varying degrees to *The Comedy of Errors*, *The Tempest*, *The Winter's Tale* and *Pericles*. All have a definitely mediaeval flavour, and the " duke of Athens " suggests rather a duke of Burgundy of the house of Valois. The Manchester production of the *Dream*, directed by Oscar Barrett and Robert Courtneidge, was beautifully designed by the late C. Wilhelm in elaborate ancient Greek style, and it is quite usual for the play—apart from the fairy element—to be still so presented. On reflection many spectators must be conscious of the incompatibility of Theseus and his court in chiton and chlamys with Oberon, Titania and their train on the one hand, on the other with Bottom and Co. By borrowing the " mortals " of the story, not from red-figured vases, but from mediaeval miniatures, the *mise en scène* would gain enormously in homogeneity. There are a number of well-known illuminated MSS. any one of which would supply all the material required for designing the non-fairy element : the *Très riches Heures* of John, Duke of Berry (Chantilly Museum), the *Grimani Breviary* (Marciana, Venice) or—best of all, perhaps—the twin codices *Theseis* and *Le cuer d'amour espris* at Vienna. The *Theseis* in particular, a masterpiece of the miniaturist's art, has the interest of showing us expressly the mediaeval conception of the age of Theseus.[1] As for the " clowns " that figure in

[1] Vienna, Nationalbibliothek, MS. 2617. Described and fully illustrated in *Jahrbuch der kunsthistorischen Sammlungen*, etc., Vienna, Vol. XIV. *Le cuer* . . . etc. (Vienna MS. 2597) is analysed in Vol. XI. The superb colour plates of Smital and Winkler's edition of 1928 are invaluable costume material.

these as in others of the plays, the innumerable calendar-pictures that embellish nearly every " Book of Hours " of the 14th to 16th centuries afford an ample supply of models on which to draw.

The Tempest is far too unsubstantial a story to be hedged in by any hard and fast restrictions. In this and the remaining plays artistic licence may claim to range pretty widely. The " vext Bermoothës ", the seaboard of Bohemia and kindred climes must be largely a law unto themselves, and it is for the individual designer to interpret it. One condition only would I venture to impose : the several features should form an harmonious whole. It is quite allowable to give to each production a vaguely " mediaeval " character, provided that there is no incongruity between isolated details : cup-hilted rapiers are as alien to the Middle Ages and Renaissance as aeroplanes to the South African war. If you are exact in one detail, then everything else in the *mise en scène* must agree with it. I have seen a clergyman in a mediaeval play decked out with " Geneva bands " of the late 17th century, and Hamlet in a slashed Albert Dürer bonnet confronting Claudius in a Carolingian crown. At the risk of passing for a pedantic prig, I venture to record my opinion that these things are altogether out of place except in burlesque.[1]

51. English sailor: very loose jerkin or coat-like garment with slit and lace holes at neck; baggy slops, falling ruff, thrum hat. Late 16th century.
Cerare Vecellis, *Habiti Antichi e Moderni*. Venice, 1598.

I have noted the importance to the designer of knowing in advance the personalities he is called upon to clothe. The better he is acquainted with them and not merely with their physique—the more successful are likely to be the results. Their unconsciousness of personal defects may be no more a drawback than over-sensitiveness. And this is apt to call for the nicest tact on the designer's part. The wider his acquaintance with the modes of the period, the more readily can he cope with difficulties ; for the better will he realize the endless variety at his disposal, and hence be best qualified to take *intelligent liberties* with his material.

[1] For 16th-century sailors, for instance, see Figure 6 for a sea-officer, and Figure 51 for a seaman.

CHAPTER VII

ON AVAILABLE SOURCES AND THEIR SELECTION

It is impossible in a single volume of modest size and moderate price to convey to the budding designer or producer even a tithe of the information which he will need in dealing at all adequately either with costume-plays at large or Shakespeare in particular. The most one can hope to do—and very imperfectly at that—is to guide his footsteps into the likeliest paths to lead him to success. The reader will find included in this little book a select Bibliography of Costume and Armour ; with a certain emphasis on the word " select ". For whether you collect books or pictures, quality is more important than quantity, though you can hardly have too much material provided it is of the right sort. To accumulate pell-mell good, bad and indifferent matter will only result in wholesale confusion in the collector's mind. It would have been an easy matter to treble or quadruple our catalogue. In effect this would have amounted in part to a deal of idle repetition, since a large proportion of modern costume-books are mere uncritical compilations—" cribbed " from earlier works, without adding anything of value to their predecessors. A really useful working-library should—to begin with at any rate—eschew everything not likely to be of definite use.

That admirable antiquary the late Maurice Maindron once declared : " I shall never cease to correct my mistakes so long as I am alive, in other words so long as I am learning " ; and I am personally acquainted with two distinguished scholars, octogenarians, who are living examples of this spirit. Such zeal is scarcely to be expected from the great majority of researchers : I merely instance it as a warning to the numerous " costume writers " who from insufficient data venture to set themselves up as qualified guides and mentors to their fellows. After all the public, which ultimately pays the piper, has a right to expect its money's worth of honest goods. This applies to designers and (in a minor degree) producers. The least one is entitled to demand from them is that they should be reasonably thorough and wholly sincere: what the French describe in one word as *sérieux*.

Your ideal costume expert should be a man of attainments, combining under the same hat antiquary, artist, scholar, linguist, critic—and tailor; but this of course is a paragon hardly to be looked for in our imperfect world. While one cannot reasonably demand of the student much practical knowledge of the tailor's art, he will find a theoretical acquaintance with the principles of "cut" and drapery an invaluable aid in deciphering the naïve productions of primitive art. It will be no less worth his while to have at least a smattering of languages other than English and to miss no opportunity to consult the art of the past for possible material. Above all he should cultivate a nice sense of date, never neglect verifying references and keep his acquired material up to date by frequent revision and correction in the light of fuller knowledge.

As to available first-hand sources I can only repeat what I have said elsewhere[1]: "The artistic material at our disposal is practically endless; almost daily new stores of information become available in the form of reproductions of every form of art: books are constantly appearing on this or that artist, school of painting, engraving, sculpture, illumination and what not. Art magazines, illustrated catalogues, even dealers' advertisements, are full of material." In fact on re-reading the "Introduction" from which this passage is culled, I find it still expresses what I wish here to convey so aptly that I would venture to refer the reader to the whole of it, merely reprinting now one paragraph as to literary evidence.

"It is impossible, in view of the vast field of research available, to advise the reader as to literary sources of information. Practically any of the old romances, chronicles, *fabliaux* are likely to afford him useful material. Nowadays a great number of these are increasingly available in modern type, carefully edited by competent scholars. The French texts should not be neglected considering the close connection between their country and ours for many centuries. From the close of the 14th century we can depend more fully on our own native resources, Chaucer, Lydgate, the Paston letters, etc.; the Tudor dramatists and satirists, diarists, writers like Stubbes, Peacham and Bulwer; later essayists, letter-writers and biographers, to say nothing of notices in the contemporary news-sheets, give us plenty to bite on. Wardrobe-accounts, wills and inventories are full of valuable matter. Dictionaries too and glossaries had been in use for

[1] *Short History of Costume and Armour*, Vol. I, pt. 1, *Introduction.*

some time, and one way and another we shall not run short of fuel. Occasionally—though this very rare—illustrations accompany the text."

To which it may be useful to add that unexpected light upon details of costume may fall from the least obvious sources : e.g. books on botany, Markham's *Compleat Gentleman*, Nashe's *Have with you to Saffron Walden* (in which " round hose " are expressly delineated), etc.

Unless the organization producing a Shakespearian play have " lashings " of leisure, means and talent at their disposal, it is not fair to exact of amateur or provincial companies a very high standard in the staging of period ; since their costumes and properties will generally have to be improvised or borrowed from stock (i.e. in most cases hired from a theatrical costumier). Those who aim high and wish to create their own *mise en scène*, yet, remote from important libraries and museums, dispose of limited funds, might well invest in a copy of Miss Lucy Barton's *Historic Costume* or Miss Margot Lister's *Costume*, either of which they will find a useful stand-by. This with Fairholt's *English Costume* (Dillon's edition), Mrs Morse's *Elizabethan Pageantry* and (for ancient military gear) either Demmin's *Arms and Armour* or Hewitt's *Ancient Armour and Weapons* will form a useful foundation for a permanent working library, to which, as means allow, may be added the writings of C. R. Beard, C. Buttin, Sir J. Mann and Herbert Norris, James Laver, and the Cunningtons. To those—they are apt to be more numerous than they admit—who can muster up between them a sufficient knowledge of French, I would recommend Quicherat's *Costume en France*, and to German-speakers either Quincke's *Handbuch der Kostümkunde* or Köhler's *Allgemeine Trachtenkunde*. As a model of thoroughness and pattern of how a study of a *particular* period of costume should be carried out, I have no hesitation in citing Adrien Harmand's *Jeanne d'Arc*. The designer or producer desirous of putting on *Henry IV*, *Henry V* or *Henry VI* (*part I*) will find it a veritable treasury, as practical as it is scholarly ; for, so far as masculine costume (civil or military) is concerned, there is hardly a working problem that confronts him, but he will find the detailed solution ready worked out for him here ; its only serious lack is a good index.

But for more pretentious stage-productions, above all for films where realism is more or less taken for granted, more extensive and intensive research is clearly indicated, such as can hardly be undertaken outside of London. Here only will you find practically everything you are likely to need : in the various museums, the British Museum and South Kensington libraries and print-rooms. From the pictorial point of view it is unlikely you will anywhere else find a field of work comparable to the magnificent Witt Library of photographs and reproductions. This, by the generosity of Sir Robert and Lady Witt, its creators, is a national possession housed by the Courtauld Institute of 20 Portman Square.

It is therefore chiefly to those who can avail themselves in person or by deputy of London's resources that my book, with its rather ambitious programme, is addressed. Only here will they be able to verify practically all their data and add to them.

At the end of Chapter IV of the costume of Shakespeare's age I have given a list of painters whose work may fruitfully be studied in illustration of the subject. All these and innumerable others the student will find reproduced *en masse*, in the Witt Library ; so sensibly arranged that he can establish immediate contact with the artist desired.

I have long held that for purposes of explanation—so far as concrete objects are concerned—the most summary of sketches by one who knows his job is apt to be more revealing than pages of descriptive prose. Yet, for a proper understanding of the points revealed, the pictorial side of the matter will yield full fruit *only* in the light of intelligent literary comment : the two are complementary. Only by combining both will the student really grasp what he is looking at : its " anatomy ", as it were.

One cannot overstress the importance of verifying references. Thus Mrs Morse in *Elizabethan Pageantry* follows Fairholt (Dillon's edition, vol. I, page 255, note 2) in quoting Peacham as writing : "... long stockings without garters, then were the Earl of Leicester's fashion, and theirs who had the handsomest leg ". Actually the original runs " . . . round breeches not much unlike St Omer's onions, *whereto* the long stocking without garters was *joined, which was* then the Earl of Leicester's . . . " etc., a very different and far more comprehensive statement.

CHAPTER VIII

ODDS AND ENDS

Short of writing a *catalogue raisonné* of modern costume-books it is hardly practicable to guide the reader in avoiding certain " authorities ". In passing, however, we might say : mistrust all authors who repeat the old story of the long-toed shoes chained up to the knees or date the steeple crowned *hennin* much earlier than 1460.

Always take care to verify and re-verify your *dates* ; test your *data* incessantly and from every angle.

The following hints refer principally to Elizabethan costume :

Don't wear heels to your shoes prior to James I.

Don't wear your cloak, like a train, pinned to the shoulder-blades ; and don't have it made of crumply material : it should (especially the short " cape ") *flare* stiffly.

Don't have *any* creases in your doublet, any more than you would in a properly cut dress-coat.

Don't think that correct *clothes* are all sufficient : the effect will be ruined without the corresponding *period make-up*.

Don't be extravagant with broad gold and silver lace trimmings (gimp especially) ; this tendency is only a heritage of the time when actors were " rogues and vagabonds ".

Don't, if you wear a morion, tilt it forward : nothing looks sillier ; and don't forget it is essentially an *infantry* helmet.

Don't appear on full-dress occasions minus cloak (or gown). This does not apply to military or menial costume.

Don't wear boots indiscriminately. Shoes, not boots, are the ceremonial wear till 1600.

Don't go in for variety of wardrobe (for the one rôle) without a definite reason. One effective costume, be it never so sober, outvies a dozen un-meaning changes.

Don't forget the value of black—intelligently used ; on the other hand don't abuse it.

N.B.—All black costumes need careful treatment.[1] Especially in velvet or fine cloth, they are apt at a short distance to be blurred into a mere flat silhouette, within which all details of form are lost, unless picked out by contrast of material or trimming. In acting on this hint, avoid equally jet and bright silver. The former, although beloved of the Victorian age and still a stand-by of many designers, does *not* make for definition of form : it merely lets you down with a fidgety effect. Especially under the strong studio lights, both jet and bright silver—spangles above all—form a kind of flashing halo, with resulting loss of clean outline. Mat silver is free from this objection.

Don't, because blue is " too sweet for words ", imagine it specially suitable for Elizabethan court wear : Elizabethans regarded it as a flunkey's colour. Sky blue and pink is definitely not an Elizabethan harmony—nor in contemporary Europe.

Don't ever wear a broad leather belt with a large buckle in front girt horizontally round your middle : it is of course quite correct for *The Pirates of Penzance*.

Don't, ladies, be content with modern undies alone—to get the effect and " hang " of Elizabethan clothes the correct petticoats and farthingales must be worn.

Don't believe the current legend that the present uniform of the Yeomen of the Guard " descends in unbroken line from the days of Henry VIII ". On this misleading tradition see C. R. Beard's article on the subject in *Archæol. Journ.* 2 Series, Vol. XXXII (1928), pp. 91-148.

And while we are on the subject, a word of warning upon " popular " traditions in general. Never take their truth for granted : they have a disheartening way of collapsing in the witness-box. Yet, as in the case of the notorious Tichborne claimant, " the great heart of the public " continues to believe in them, and the Black Prince's *black* armour, the crossed legs of " crusaders " on tombs, " banded mail ", etc., still have their supporters.

Except in actual battle-scenes, military parades and musters, one should not be prodigal of armour. In most other settings—in camp or guardroom—you will not only be more correct, but more novel and effective, if you are content with military underwear relieved with gussets, etc., of mail and a steel gorget.

[1] " Hamlet " of course strikes traditionally an isolated note.

Let your slashes look like slashes, not like stuck-on open jam tarts. (Still a common fault in 1973.)

Decolleté shoes with a single strap and button across the top of the instep are quite alien to Elizabethan costume.

In actual costumes of stage or screen one of the commonest defects is disregard of the *proportions* in details as given in the model: e.g. in the relative size, number and spacing of trimmings. Skimpiness in cloaks, gowns, etc., is another prevalent fault, or *per contra* undue floppiness: often both occur together. When you are fortunate enough to come across a good, characteristic model (design), copy it with Chinese fidelity. In this connection note how widely the so-called "Mary Queen of Scots" (Mary Stuart) hoods on stage or screen differ from the real thing: the latter is as neat and compact as the former are "all over the shop". (Pl 8.)

Clothes that "fit where they touch" are only excusable in stock wardrobes. Don't be less exacting about the fit and cut of "costume" than is the ordinary well-dressed man who is prepared to pay good money to a leading West End tailor.

Try to get the right "feel" of your costume. If the designer and costumier understand their job, it should help you in expressing your part. Even the most unpromising modes can be, with comparatively few exceptions, adapted to the individual wearer, without sacrificing the character of the period.

Let not the actor protest against the costume allotted him without giving it a fair "try out" in front of a pier-glass (or, better still, a hinged three-leaved mirror). The effect will often be to convert him entirely.

The designer should, before composing his colour-scheme, have a clear vision of the particular lighting to which his dresses will have to stand up. For instance a very full amber lighting will inevitably kill every colour save black and the strongest reds. Therefore if yellow light is to be used we would suggest that the courtly costumes of an Elizabethan setting should ring the changes on black, and white (sparingly relieved with gold and silver) and an occasional note of red. Let your scenic *repoussoirs*—tapestries, curtains, upholstery, etc.—be as varied in colour as you like within reason: they will suffer comparatively little from being flooded with a strong amber light, their varied colours just serving unobtrusively to break up the monotony of the all-pervading yellow—a rôle to which the persons of the play should not be reduced: *their* figures should stand out.

However, with the versatility and flexibility of modern stage lighting

PLATE 8

Pointed bodice with low neckline, slightly arched ; plain close sleeves ; open lace ruff and ruffles; Mary Stuart hood and wired head-rail falling over shoulders. 1578.

Mary, Queen of Scots. P. Oudry.
National Portrait Gallery, London.

the costume designer should not be limited in his choice of colours. It is hardly necessary to say that each costume must be in harmony with any others on stage at the same time, and must also complement the decor of the set.

Note finally that the greatest of the old masters are by no means always the most reliable witnesses to contemporary modes. Documentary value is often in inverse ratio to aesthetic merit.

All of which random remarks are the outcome of first-hand experience.

GENERAL BIBLIOGRAPHY

COSTUME, GENERAL AND PARTICULAR

BARTON, Lucy : *Historic Costume for the Stage*, 1937. A. & C. Black.

BOEHN, M. von : *Modes and Manners* (transl. with notes by Joan Joshua), vols. I–II, 1932. Harrap.

HARTLEY, Dorothy : *Mediæval Costume and Life*, 1931. Batsford.

KELLY, F. M. and R. SCHWABE : *Historic Costume* (2nd ed.), 1929. Batsford.
Short History of Costume and Armour, 1931. Batsford.

LINTHICUM, M. C. : *Costume in the Drama of Shakespeare and his contemporaries*, 1936. Oxford University Press.

LONSDALE and TARVER : *Illustrations of Mediæval Costume*, 1874.

MASON, Rupert and Geo. SHERINGHAM : *Robes of Thespis*, 1928.

MORSE, H. K. : *Elizabethan Pageantry* (*The Studio* Special Spring Number, 1934).

NORRIS, Herbert : *Costume and Fashion*, Vol. III, 1938. Dent.

PLANCHÉ, J. R. : *British Costume*, 1874.

FRENCH

ENLART, Camille : *Manuel d'Archéologie française:* iii—" Le Costume ".

GAY, Victor : *Glossaire archéologique* . . . etc.

HARMAND, Adrien : *Jeanne d'Arc.*

PARMENTIER, A. : *Album historique.*

QUICHERAT, J. : *Le costume en France.*

RENAN, Ary : *Le Costume.*

VIOLLET-LE DUC : *Dictionnaire du mobilier français* (6 vols. III–IV Costume, V–VI Arms and Armour).

Paris—SOCIÉTÉ DE L'HISTOIRE DU COSTUME. Publications generally.

GERMAN, ETC.

BESIER, J. H. der Kinderen : *Mode Metamorphosen. De Kleedij . . . in de XVIe eeuw.*

DE JONGE, C. H. (in *Oud Holland*, vols. 36 and 37) *Bijdrage tot de Kennis van de Kleederdracht* . . . etc.

FALKE, J. von : *Kostümgeschichte der Kulturvölker.*

KÖHLER, Bruno : *Allgemeine Trachtenkunde.*

MASNER, Karl : *Kostümausstellung.*

QUINCKE, W. : *Handbuch der Kostümkunde.*
WEISS, Hermann : *Kostümkunde.*
Munich. GESSELSCHAFT FÜR HISTORISCHE WAFFEN-UND KOSTÜMKUNDE. *Zeitschrift.*

ARMS AND ARMOUR

COSSON, C. A. de : *On Gauntlets* (in *Archæol. Journ.* xli, 1884).
and W. BURGESS : *Catalogue of Helmets and Mail* (*ibid.* xxxvii, 1880).
DEMMIN, A. : *Arms and Armour* (transl. by C. C. Black).
DILLON, H. A. (Viscount) : *Armour Notes* (in *Archæol. Journ.*).
FFOULKES, C. C. : *The Armourer and his Craft.*
MANN, Sir J. : Writings generally in *Archæologia* lxxix (1929), lxxx (1930), etc., *Archæological Journal* . . . etc.
TRAPP, Oswald (Count) : *Armoury of the Castle of Churburg* (transl. with a Preface by Sir J. Mann).

FRENCH

BUTTIN, Charles : Writings *passim*, notably *Le Gisant d'Ulrich de Werdt—Le Guet de Genève—Notes sur les Armures à l'Épreuve*, etc. All lucid, scholarly and packed with information.
DUYSE, Hermann van : *Catalogue de . . . la Porte de Hal* (Introduction).
MAINDRON, M. : *Les Armes.*

GERMAN, ETC.

BÖHEIM, W. : *Handbuch der Waffenkunde.*

Of Armour an unusually full bibliography is appended by Mr F. H. Cripps-Day to vol. V of LAKING : *Record of European Armour.*

All of these and a veritable host of other works on costume generally are to be found in the libraries of the British Museum and the South Kensington Museum. In the latter may be seen an excellent (typed) catalogue of their whole collection of costume-books. In addition to these one may profitably refer there to the bibliographies of FR. VON LIPPERHEIDE, R. COLAS, and MONRO and COOK, *Costume Index.*

Not wishing to repeat myself, I would refer my readers to the *Iconography* appended to Kelly and Schwabe's *Short History*. For mid-15th century costumes nothing could better the sumptuous edition by Smital and Winkler (a marvel of Austrian colour-printing) of King René's MSS. *Le Cuer d'Amour espris* and *La Théséide* at Vienna : see at South Kensington under heading : VIENNA-NATIONALBIBLIOTHEK.

Otherwise I think the aforesaid brief " Iconographies " sum up fairly effectively what suggestions I have to offer as to available artistic sources of information. Best of all, of course, as opportunity offers, is to study the original works at first hand in museums, public and private collections, exhibitions, etc.

ADDITIONAL WORKS

(Published in London, unless otherwise stated)

ENGLAND AND EUROPE GENERALLY

AUERBACH, E. : *Nicholas Hilliard.* Routledge & Kegan Paul, 1961.

CAMDEN, C. : *The Elizabethan Woman.* Cleaver-Hume Press Ltd., 1952.

CUNNINGTON, C. W. and P. E. : *Handbook of English Medieval Costume.* Faber & Faber, 1952.

Handbook of English Costume in the 16th Century. Faber & Faber, 1954.

Handbook of English Costume in the 17th Century. Faber & Faber, 1955.

and C. BEARD: *A Dictionary of English Costume.* A. & C. Black, 1960.

CUNNINGTON, P. E. and C. LUCAS (with Chapters by A. D. MANSFIELD) : *Occupational Costume in England.* A. & C. Black, 1967.

FAIRHOLT, F. W. : *Costume in England.* Various editions.

HAMILTON HILL, M. and P. A. BUCKNELL : *The Evolution of Fashion. Pattern and Cut from 1066 to 1930.* Batsford, London, 1967, and Reinhold Publishing Corporation, New York, 1968.

HOUSTON, M. G. : *Ancient Greek, Roman and Byzantine Costume,* 2nd Edn. A. & C. Black, 1947.

KÖHLER, CARL : *A History of Costume,* edited by Emma von Sichart, 1928 edn. republished 1963 by Dover Publications Inc., New York. (Mostly Continental fashions.)

KYBALOVA, L., HERBENOVA, O. and M. LAMAROVA : *The Pictorial Encyclopedia of Fashion.* Paul Hamlyn, London, and Crown Publishers Inc., New York, 1968. (Mostly Continental fashions.)

LA MAR, V. A. : *English Dress in the Age of Shakespeare.* Folger Shakespeare Library, Washington, 1958.

LAVER, J. : *Clothes.* (Pleasures of Life Series.) Burke, 1952. (Many extracts from original sources.)

LISTER, M. : *Costume : an Illustrated Survey from Ancient Times to the 20th Century.* Herbert Jenkins, 1967.

MACLAGAN, Sir E. : *The Bayeux Tapestry.* King Penguin Book, 1943.

REYNOLDS, G. : *Elizabethan and Jacobean, 1558–1625.* (Costume of the Western World Series.) Harrap, 1951.

RUBENS, A. : *A History of Jewish Costume.* Valentine Mitchell, 1967.

SMITH, L. Baldwin : *Horizon Book of the Elizabethan World.* Paul Hamlyn and The American Heritage Publishing Co. Inc., 1967. (A good background to the period and a lot of costume illustrations, English and Continental.)

WEBSTER, G. : *The Roman Army.* Grosvenor Museum, Chester.

FRANCE

PITON, C. : *Le Costume Civil en France du XIIIe au XIX siècle.* Flammarion, 1913.

WEIGERT, R. A.: *Pourpoint et vertugadins.* (Costumes et modes d'autrefois.) Editions Rombaldi, 1958.

GERMANY

DRESDEN STAATLICHE KUNSTSAMMLUNGEN. *Historische Prunkkleidung*, 1963.

HOLLAND

DE VRIES, A. B. : *Het Noord-Nederlandsh portret in de tweede helft van de 16e. eeuw.* Amsterdam, 1934.

ITALY

BENTIVEGNA, F. C. : *Abbigliamento e costume nella pittura Italiana.* Vol. I, *15th and 16th centuries.* Carlo Bertetti, Rome, 1962.

SPAIN

READE, B. : *The Dominance of Spain, 1550–1666.* (Costume of the Western World Series.) Harrap, 1951.

ARMS AND ARMOUR

BLAIR, CLAUDE : *European Armour.* Batsford, 1958.
European and American Arms. Batsford, 1962.

MANN, SIR J.: *Arms and Armour in England.* H.M.S.O., 1968.
(A useful booklet with some illustrations of the 16th and 17th centuries.)

STAGECRAFT GENERALLY

GREEN, RUTH : *The Wearing of Costume.* Pitman, 1966. (Many useful hints and ideas on the management of historical clothes.)

NICOLL, ALLARDYCE : *The Development of the Theatre.* Harrap, various editions. (This discusses the contemporary costuming of Shakespeare's plays, and also reproduces the Dialogues of Leoni di Somi (c 1565) on stage management, costume, etc.)

INDEX

Page numbers in *italics* indicate an illustration in the text, but in the case of articles of clothing, where written reference is made on the same page as an illustration ordinary type is generally used.
Items of armour are indexed under " Armour ".
TITLES of the PLAYS appear under " PLAYS ".

Actor, 78, 81, 88
Aglets, Aiglets, 20, 59
Alençon (Anjou), Duke of, 18
" Antick " costume, 15
Apron, 60, 63, 66, *100*
Armour, 11, 45, 93
  parts of, 71, 72
    Almain collar, 71
    Arming cap, 66
    Arming doublet, 20, 65
    Basnet, 66
    Beaver, 66, 67
    Buffe, 67, 68
    Burgonet, *67*, 68
    Cabasset, 68
    Corslet, 69, pl. 3
    Cuirass, *27*, 65, 69, 71, pl. 3
    Elbow gauntlet, 70, 71
    Gorget, *36*, 45, 69, 71, pl. 2, pl. 3
    Greaves, 66, 71
    Hauberk, 91
    Lames, 66
    Monnion, 70, 71
    Pauldrons, 20, 69, 70, 71, pl. 3
    Sabaton, 66, 71
    Skull, 66
    Tasses, 69, 70, 71, pl. 3
    Vambraces, 20, 66, 69, 70, 71, pl. 3
    Ventaille, 67
    Visor, 66, 67
  Brigandine, 69, 70, 97, 98
  Cap-a-pie, 64, 65, 86
  field, 65
  Headpieces, 66
  Helmet, close, 66, *67*
  Jack, 69, 70
  Morion, *67*, 68, 70
  Sallet, 68
  Stage, 86, 91
  Types of, 65, 66

Bands, 36, 37, 57, pl. 5
Bandstrings, 36, 37, pl. 5
Barette, *101*
Base-coat, 35
Beards, 43, 91
  Forked—swallow-tailed, 43
  Marquisetto, *42*, 43
  Pickedevant, 43
  Spade, *36*, 43
  Stiletto, 43
Belt, 31, 33; *see also* Girdle
Betterton, 12
Bodice, 48, 63
Bodies, 49
Bombast, *see* Padding
Bonnet, *29*, 40, 41, *62*, pl. 4
Boot hose, 29
Boots, 39, 40, 66
Bosom, 49, 57
Braid, 31, 32
Breasts, 50, 57

Breech, 25
Breeches, 25, 27
Buff jerkin, 30, 45
Bum-roll, 47, *49*, 58
Burbage, 13
Buskins, *see* Boots
Buttons, 19, 23, 24, 49, 52

Cane, 47
Canes, 45
Canions, *23*, 26, *29*, 29
Cap:
 Buttoned, 40
 Flat, *33*, 40
 Monmouth, 42
 Skull, 42, *95*
 Statute, 40
Cape, *26*, 31, 33, 50, 62
Cassock, 33, *34*, 50, pl. 4
Caul, 53, *101*
Chammer, Shamew, 34
Chemise, 49, 57, 58
Chopines, 56
Cloak:
 Men's, 21, *23*, *26*, 31, 32, *62*
  Dutch, 31, 32
  French, 31, *31*, 32, pl. 1
  Spanish, 31
 Women's, 50, *60*
Cloak-bag breeches, 28
Clocks, 28, 59
Coat, 35, 50
Cockers, 40
Cod-piece, 27, 28, *61*, pl. 2, pl. 4
Coif, 42, *43*, 53
Collar:
 Bodice, 49
 Cloak, 31
 Doublet, 22, 37
 Gown, 33, 52
 Mandilion, 34
 Shirt, 35
 See also Band, Ruff, etc.
Colley-westonward, 34
Colours, 17, 18, 32, 37, 38, 59, 63, 91

Corsets, 49, 52, 58
Cosmetics, 60
Costume, 78, 79, 81
Costumier, 16, 77, 78
Costuming plays, 12, 82
Cross-gartering, 29, 102
Cuffs, 37, *48*, 57, pl. 1, pl. 5
Cut, 16, 92, 107
Cuts, 19

Dagger, 25, 43, 44, 84, 86
Dancing, 21
Décolletage, Décolleté, 49, 50, 57, 58, pl. 6, pl. 8
Decoration, 24, 26, 27, 30, 31, 32, 33, 35, 37, 38, 40, 51, 52
Designer, 81, 82, 89, 112
Detachable sleeves, 24
Doublet, 18, 21, 24, *25*, pl. 1, pl. 2, pl. 4
 Arming, 20, 65
Drawers:
 Men's, 37
 Women's, 48, *56*, 59
Duel, 84
Dutch, 22, 28, 32, 49, 61
 Breeches, *27*
 Waist, 50

Elizabeth I, Queen, 21, 23, 50, pl. 6
Embroidery, 24, 28, 31, 32, 35, 37, 42, 45, 50, 51, 53, 57, 58, 59, pl. 7

Falling band, 35, 36, 57, 63, pl. 1
False hair, 55
Fan, *48*, *50*, 59, *60*
Farthingale, 47, *48*, *49*, *50*, 57, *60*
Fastenings, 19, 22, 30
Fire-arms, 64
Flounce, 48
Footwear, 38, 39, 56
Forepart, 49, *50*, 51, 52
Fore sleeves, 52
France, French, 32, 47, 49, 61, *61*, 62, 92, 99
French hose, 25
Frounce, 48
Fur, 60, 63, *103*

Gaberdine, 34
Galligaskins, Galligascoines, 28
Galoshes, 39
Garrick, 12, *13*
Garters, *23*, *27*, 28, *29*, 59, *87*
Gauntlet, 45
German, Germany, 19, 26, *26*, 61, 63, 93, 100, *103*
Girdle, 25, 43, 60, pl. 1, pl. 2, pl. 5
Girdlestead, 25
Gloves, 45, 59
Golilla, 36, pl. 5
Gorget, *36*, 45, 69, 71, pl. 2, pl. 3
" Gothick " costume, 13
Gown:
  Men's, 21, 33, *62*, *103*
  Women's, 48, 51, 52, *54*
Greek costume, 90
Guards, 20, 32, 52

Hair, 42, 53, 55
  Dye, 55, 60
Half shirt, 38
Handkerchiefs, 45, 59
Hangers, 25, 44, 86, *87*
Hanging sleeves, *see* Sleeves
Hat, 21, 40, 42
  Copotain, *17*, 41, *87*
  Men's, *27*, 70
  Sugar loaf, 42
  Thrum, 42, *105*
  Women's, 54
Head-dress, Women's, 53, 54, 55, pl. 6, pl. 8
Headrail, 54, pl. 6, pl. 8
Head wear, 40
Hennin, 92
Hood, 31, *43*, 50
  Arched, 53, *54*
  French, 53
  Mail, 91
  Mary Stuart, 53, *60*, pl. 8
Hooks and eyes, 19, 23, 49
Hose, 18, 21, 25, 59

Irving, Sir Henry, 80, 81
Italy, Italian, 40, 49, 56, 59, 63, 87, 93, 98

Jacket:
  Men's, *see* Jerkin
  Women's, 50, 58, pl. 7
James I, King, 18, 21, *27*
Jerkin, 18, 21, *23*, *24*, *27*, *29*, 30, *95*, pl. 5
Jewels, 24, 32, 42, 46, 51, 56, 60
Jewish costume, *100*, *101*
Jonson, Ben, 11

Kirtle, 51, 59, pl. 7
Knickers, *see* Drawers, women's

Lace, 29, 31, 32, 35, 36, 38, 50, 53, 56, 57
Laces, Lacing, 23, 66
Lap mantle, 50
Leather, 24, 25, 30, 39, 40, 65, 66, 69
Lining, 25, 26
Livery, 18, 20, 34
Long-stockinged hose, 25
Love lock 43

Make-up, 88, 110
Mandilion, 33, 34
Masks, 45, 60
Materials, 17, 24, 25, 28, 30, 32, 33, 35, 37, 38, 41, 42, 45, 50, 53, 57, 58, 59, 91
Mediaeval, 12, 15, 83, 91
Middle Ages, 14
Military, 18, 19, 20, 26, 34, 45, 65, 85
Mirror, 59, 60
Modern dress, 12, 15
Mourning, 53, 54
Moustache, 43, 68, 91
Muff, 45, *48*, *52*, 60
Muffler, 60

Netherlands, 28, 49, 61
Nether stocks, 25, 28
Night cap, 38, 42, pl. 5
Night gown, 33, 42
Night shirt, 38

Official dress, 20
Open breeches, 28
Open hose, 28
Overshoes, 39

Padding and stiffening, 22, 23, 26, 47, 49, 50
Panes, paning, 26, *27*, 44, *61*, pl. 2, pl. 3, pl. 4
Pantoffles, 39, 56
Partlet, 49, pl. 6
Pattens, 39
Peascod-belly, 22, pl. 2, pl. 3
Pen-case, 25
Perfume, 58
Petticoat, 35, 52, 59
Pickadils, 22, *24*, *27*, 36, 37, 40, 45, 63, pl. 3
Pinking, 19, 24, 25, *27*, 40, 50, *62*, pl. 2
Plays:
  All's well that ends well, 85, 99
  Anthony and Cleopatra, 89, 90
  As you like it, 104
  Comedy of Errors, 104
  Coriolanus, 85, 89, 90
  Cymbeline, 93
  Hamlet, 12, 56, 67, 94
  Henry IV, V, VI (Part I), 91
  Henry VI (Parts II and III), 92
  Henry VIII, 81, 89, 92
  Julius Caesar, 89, 90
  King John, 89, 91
  King Lear, 94
  Love's Labour's Lost, 99
  Macbeth, 12, *13*, 95
  Measure for Measure, 103
  Merchant of Venice, 100
  Merry Wives of Windsor, 103
  Midsummer Night's Dream, 104
  Much Ado about Nothing, 99
  Othello, 80
  Pericles, 104
  Richard II, 91
  Richard III, 12, 89, 92
  Romeo and Juliet, 13, 97
  Taming of the Shrew, 101
  Tempest, 104, 105
  Timon of Athens, 89
  Troilus and Cressida, 85, 89
  Twelfth Night, 102
  Winters Tale, 104
Pluderhose, 26
Pockets, 27, 28
Points, 19, 20, 22, 23, *24*, 25, 29, 38, 39, 59
Poker, Pokingstick, Setting stick, 36
Pomander, 60
Producer, 80, 81
Puffs, 19, 26, 49
Pullings-out, 19
Purse, 25, 60

Querpo, 21

Raquette, 55
Ratepenade, *Ratepenache*, 55
Rebato, 36, *57*
Renaissance, 14, 83
Ribbon, 56, pl. 5
Riding coat, 34
Roll, 24
Roman costume, 90
Round hose, 25
Ruff, 22, *23*, *27*, 35, 36, 37, *48*, 57, pl. 2, pl. 3, pl. 4, pl. 6, pl. 8
  Cartwheel, 49, 57
  Falling, 37
  Hand, 37
Ruffles, 37, pl. 2, pl. 3, pl. 4, pl. 6, pl. 8

Safeguard, 50
Sailor, *105*
Sash or Scarf, *27*, 33, 45, 68
Sets, 36
Shamew, *see* Chammer
Shirt, 35
Shoes, 38, *39*, 56, 66, pl. 3
Shoe-roses, 39, *39*, *95*
Siddons, Mrs, 12
Skirt, 48, 50, 51, 59, pl. 7
  Doublet, 22, pl. 1, pl. 2
  Jerkin, 30, pl. 5
Slashes, Slashing, 19, 24, 49, 50, 51, *61*, *62*, 63, pl. 2, pl. 5
Sleeves, 20, 23, 33, 49, *51*, 52, 62
  Bishop, 23, 49, 50
  Cannon, 23, 50
  Farthingale, 24
  Hanging, 30, 31, 33, 34, *48*, 49, 50, 52

Puffed, 30, 49, *51*, 52, pl. 6
Trunk, 23, *24*, 50, pl. 1
Slops, 28, 100, *105*
Soldiers, 18
types of, *64*, 69, 70
Spain, Spanish, 17, *26*, *29*, 31, 40, 47, 49 56, 59, 61, 70, 87, 99
Spurs, 39
Standing band, 36, *48*, *50*
Starch, 37, 57
Startups, 40
Stiffening, *see* Padding
Stockings, 18, *23*, 25, 26, 28, 29, *29*, 62
Women's, 59
Stola, 91
Stomacher, 49, *50*, 52
Stripes, 19
Strossers, *see* Drawers, men's
Suit of apparel, 18
Sumptuary laws, 19
Supportasse, 36, *57*
Swiss, 26, 63
Sword, 13, 21, 25, 43, 44, 84, 86

Tabs, 22, 30
Target, 65, 70
Tassel, 32
Tippet, 33, 63
Toga, 90, 91
Trains, 51
Trousers, *see* Drawers, men's
Trunks, 25
Trunk breeches, 25
Trunk hose, *23*, 25, *27*, *29*, *87*, *95*, pl. 2, pl. 3 pl. 4, pl. 5
Tunic, Roman, 91

Under bodice, 49
Underclothes, 25
Men's, 35
Women's, 47, 48, *49*, 57, 58, 59
Underpetticoat, 47, 48, *49*, 59
Underproper, 36, *57*
Upperstocks, 25, 28

Veil, 53, 54, 63
Venetians, *18*, *24*, 27, *29*, *34*, 63
Venice, 56, *62*, 63
Verdingale, 47, 51, 63; *see also* Farthingale
Verdugo, 47
Vest, 35

Waistcoat, 35,
Women's, 50, 58
Weapons, 70, 73; *see also* Dagger, Sword
Whole-hose, 25
Widow, 53
Wings, 24, *24*, *25*, *27*, 30, 49, 50, 52, pl. 1, pl. 2, pl. 5, pl. 7